SHORT WAL

CW00402403

Lincolnshire Pubs

Brett Collier

COUNTRYSIDE BOOKS
NEWBURY, BERKSHIRE

COUNTRYSIDE BOOKS
3 Catherine Road
Newbury, Berkshire

ISBN 1 85306 423 8

*With many thanks to those Ramblers' Association
groups that made initial recommendations and to Jim
Poole who followed my original route instructions and
suggested amendments.*

Designed by Mon Mohan
Cover illustration by Colin Doggett
Photographs and maps by the author

Produced through MRM Associates Ltd., Reading
Typeset by The Midlands Book Typesetting Company, Loughborough
Printed by Woolnough Bookbinding, Irthlingborough

Contents

*There is nothing which has been contrived by man,
by which so much happiness is produced as by a good
tavern or inn.*

Samuel Johnson

Publisher's Note

We hope that you obtain considerable enjoyment from this book; great care has been taken in its preparation. However, changes of landlord and actual closures are sadly not uncommon. Likewise, although at the time of publication all routes followed public rights of way or permitted paths, diversion orders can be made and permissions withdrawn.

We cannot of course be held responsible for such diversion orders and any inaccuracies in the text which result from these or any other changes to the routes nor any damage which might result from walkers trespassing on private property. However, we are anxious that all details covering the walks and the pubs are kept up to date and would therefore welcome information from readers which would be relevant to future editions.

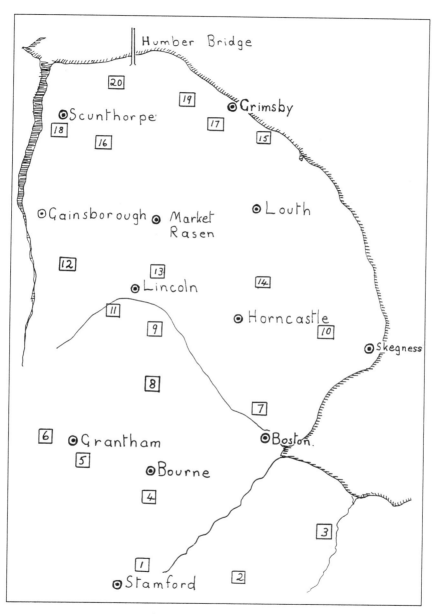

Area map showing locations of the walks.

Introduction

The real Lincolnshire is largely unexplored by the many people who just travel along its major routes. This book is intended to reveal the charms of a county of infinite variety – from the Lincoln Cliff that runs like a backbone down its length, to the lovely, rolling Wolds, now designated as an Area of Outstanding Natural Beauty (AONB), the Fens with their own special atmosphere and boundless sky, the coastal region with its nature reserves and conservation areas, and the heathland of the south.

There may be no totally secret places in Britain today, but there are certainly locations in Lincolnshire almost unknown to the general public – Skillington, just off the A1, and its valley of the Cringle Brook, Uffington and the riverbank path by the Welland where Druids once sacrificed human life, the wonder of the abbey remains in that strange, remote town of Crowland on an 'island' in the Fen or the smugglers' coast along the Humber estuary at Tetney Haven and beyond.

With the recent abolition of the South Humberside administration and the area's return to the Lincolnshire fold, it is appropriate that this book should cover what is in effect 'old' Lincolnshire from the Humber to the Wash.

The pubs were chosen partly for their geographical spread but mainly for their good ale and food and friendly atmosphere. There is obviously any number of other excellent hostelries in the county, but they may lack a suitable walk nearby. Pubs today are as much a venue for 'eating out' as for beer drinking and all the ones in this book provide good-value, interesting meals. More and more offer provision for the entertainment of children so that a pub visit can become a family occasion. One enterprising inn has a children's bar in the family room, serving soft drinks.

Most landlords readily agreed that you can leave a vehicle in their car park while walking, but it would be considerate not to park by their front entrance and it does establish a good relationship if you leave a note about your doings. A couple of landlords have already congratulated me about the courtesy of walkers who do this. These days, an unknown car left for some time in the car park without an explanation may be treated as suspicious, particularly outside normal opening hours.

Countryside officers cannot be everywhere and it would be really helpful if you could report any field path problems discovered en route to: Group Leader (Countryside), Environment Development Division Lincolnshire County Council, County Offices, Newland, Lincoln LN1 1YL. There ought not to be any, for all these walks were discussed in advance of publication with the appropriate authorities but, from time to time, field paths do get ploughed and obstructed. The law states that all public rights of way must be clearly defined to their minimum width throughout each season of the year so there are no lawful occasions where a path should not be visible on the ground. It is most important, therefore, that you attempt to remain on the correct line, for unofficial diversions around a crop can only cause confusion to later walkers trying to follow the public right of way. Remember though that grass is a crop and do try to keep in single file across a meadow. Farmers are naturally concerned about livestock and litter. Please shut gates behind you and try to make the countryside even better than you found it by picking up a piece of litter on the way. This will enhance the reputation of walkers and ensure a welcome for others who come after you.

Have a thought to being properly clothed and shod, for although Lincolnshire is lowland Britain, field paths may be muddy and rough underfoot, so stout walking shoes or boots are a sensible precaution, plus some kind of wet weather clothing – and do please remove muddy boots before going into the pub!

The sketch maps provided are quite adequate for the purpose of each walk but an Ordnance Survey map will greatly increase the pleasure and interest you gain from being away from the car on foot in the countryside. Landranger maps will tell you more about the immediate vicinity and help you to identify distant features – a steeple on the horizon and its village, the height of a hill, where the stream goes or the name of a wood and how far it is away.

The aim of the book is for you to enjoy exploring Lincolnshire. In conclusion, I hope that it will bring you hours of good walking for not only do the many miles of walks open up little-frequented countryside but they also introduce you to the high quality of food and drink that is offered in these 20 inns.

Brett Collier
Spring 1996

1 Uffington
The Bertie Arms

The Berties came to the beautiful, wooded park at Uffington in the 1670s, having bought the estate from the dissolute second Duke of Buckingham. Their name lives on in the village's popular thatched inn, built in 1681 and enlarged in the 18th century. Uffington House, one of the great mansions of Lincolnshire, was unfortunately destroyed by fire in 1904 and only the stables survived. These have now been converted into a dwelling.

The Bertie Arms has been extensively extended and remodelled but retains its old world charm.

The range of food here is impressive. There is a starter menu listing avocado and prawns with salad garnish or spicy chicken satay kebab, for example, and main courses including 'Steaks and Things' all available with interesting sauces. The sweet menu offers such delights as home-made profiteroles with chocolate sauce or 'Sloshed Chocolate' with Tia Maria. The chef's special changes weekly and could be something like sardines baked in garlic butter topped with tomato sauce and served with salad and new potatoes.

Vegetarian dishes are also available, such as feta cheese kebab served with jacket potato and salad or home-made mushroom stroganoff with rice and salad garnish. Lunchtime snacks include potato skins loaded with cheese and bacon with a yoghurt and chive dip or barbecued spare ribs served with salad. Meals are available between 12 noon and 2 pm on Monday to Friday (to 2.30 pm on Saturday) and from 6.30 pm (7.30 pm on Saturday) to 9.30 pm. On Sunday food is served without a break from 12 noon to 9.30 pm.

John Smith's Bitter, Ruddles County, Draught Bass and Mild are served in this freehouse. Stella Artois, Carling Black Label, Foster's and Miller Pilsner lager are also available, along with Blackthorn Sweet and Taunton Dry cider.

The pub is open from 12 noon to 3 pm on Monday to Friday (to 3.30 pm on Saturday) and in the evening from 6.30 pm to 12 midnight. On Sunday the hours are from 12 noon to 9.30 pm.

Telephone: 01780 63834.

How to get there: Uffington is 2 miles east of Stamford on the A16 (T), and 6 miles from Market Deeping. The Bertie Arms can be seen from the main road on the eastern edge of the village.

Parking: There is ample parking at the inn or alternatively on a side road off the main road.

Length of the walk: 2³/₄ miles or 4¹/₂ miles. OS map: Landranger 142 Peterborough and surrounding area (inn GR 064077).

The pleasant short walk takes you through a river valley by the long-abandoned Welland Canal and then over the quiet back lanes of grey-stoned Uffington village. An easily-tackled longer route leads you further along the river, across the washland to a converted mill and a weir and then into Cambridgeshire, on the other side of the river Welland, on a good firm track of the old railway line, back to an ancient bridge over the river and a return into Lincolnshire.

The Walk

Turn left out of the Bertie Arms car park along the main road for 500 yards, passing Manor Farm on your left. Where the A16 turns

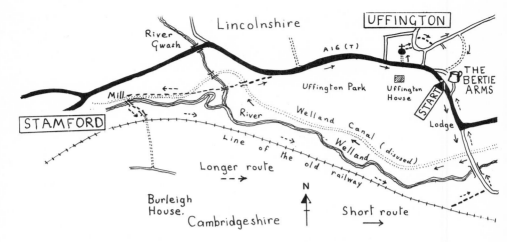

sharply left, proceed straight forward on the minor road, with the splendid gates at the lodge entrance on your right. After 300 yards on this lane and just before the ancient road bridge, turn right off the lane over the stile onto a signposted path.

Follow the line of the disused Welland Canal, with the river meandering on your left, for just over a mile.

For the shorter route, turn right at the stile, to follow the clear path up to the main road. Turn right at the A16, past the Gainsborough Lady, and continue along the road as far as the church gates. The magnificent iron gates opposite are some of the finest in the county. Turn left up the church drive and, after visiting the medieval church largely rebuilt in the 19th century, turn right again through the metal handgate at the exit from the churchyard. Turn left after leaving the churchyard for a few yards and cross the road to turn right over the school playing field through the stout handgate. Walk straight across the field to a little pathway, with a stone stile at the roadside and a thatched cottage on your right. Turn left along Casewick Lane for 250 yards and then right by Manners Close, up the attractive tarmac track, past the pond on your left and on to your starting place.

For the longer walk, turn left down to the footbridge at the stile where the shorter walk takes you back to the main road. Cross the stout bridge over the river Gwash and proceed on a clear path for about 800 yards across the washland to a stile at the side of the metal gate, with the river Welland over on your left. Turn left over the fine wooden bridge above the weir, with the old watermill upstream on your right. After crossing the concrete bridge, turn left along the tree-lined washway to follow the meanders of the river, with the old railway line on your right. After about 700 yards turn right at a stile up the railway embankment and then left to continue on a good track along the former railway bed. Burghley House and grounds may be seen and perhaps some deer, on your right. After some 900 yards, at a stile, turn left off the railway line towards the river and the old bridge, to a stile and footpath signpost on the lane. Turn left, over the road bridge and back to the main road and the Bertie Arms.

Places of interest nearby

Burghley House, Stamford, the largest and grandest house of the Elizabethan Age and the home of the Cecil family since 1565. The house and gardens are open to the public at varying times. Telephone: 01780 52451 for up-to-date information. *Stamford* itself, 'the best stone town in England', has town trails available from the Town Museum. Tourist Information Centre: 01780 55611.

Watermill on the river Welland at Stamford.

Crowland
The Abbey Hotel

Crowland, lying close to the borders of Cambridgeshire, Lincolnshire and Northamptonshire, on the edge of Deeping Fen, is remote even for this county. Only just above fen level today, it was once an island in a vast, swampy countryside. Cru-land meant soft, muddy ground and it was here that St Guthlac landed in AD 699, on a patch of dry ground above the dismal marsh, determined to live a life of solitude and austerity. He was sought out by those in need of spiritual counsel, including Ethelbald, the future King of Mercia, who later founded the abbey in remembrance of his friend and adviser. In AD 850 raiding Danes burnt the abbey and murdered Theodore, the abbot, at the altar. In 1091 a disastrous fire destroyed the rebuilt abbey and some 700 manuscripts. The Normans began reconstruction in 1113 but the building was damaged by an earthquake in 1117. The unfortunate abbey was damaged yet again by another fire in 1146 and bombarded by Cromwell in 1643. Nevertheless, part of the abbey church is still in use today as the parish church. The Abbey

Hotel was formerly the George, built in 1730 as a coaching inn. Lord Normanton, the major landowner locally and patron of the abbey in the 19th century, used to hold rent audit dinners in the hotel, where his tenants were required to pay their rents for the whole year. There used to be 34 public houses in Crowland but now there are just 5.

Today, the Abbey Hotel, lying within the shadow of the abbey in this fascinating town, is still a fine and welcoming inn. It has a smartly painted white façade with timbers picked out in black. There is a pleasant, roomy lounge bar with leatherette seating and, in season, an open fire, and a small tea room adjoins. A corridor leads you to an attractive dining room capable of seating up to 36 diners in comfort.

There is excellent bar food, such as home-made soup of the day, Brussels pâté with toast, steak and kidney pie, scampi, breaded haddock, beefburgers in a bap, turkeyburger, bacon bap, steak sandwich, various omelettes, salads and an 'All Day Breakfast'. In the dining room the starters include prawn cocktail, chicken liver pâté, mushrooms in garlic, prawn fritter dip, melons and raspberries and savoury cheese pancakes. Examples of main course fish dishes are lemon sole à la bonne femme, large breaded scampi, salmon steak and salmon en croûte. Among the beef dishes are beef Wellington, fillet of beef stroganoff and curry, and there are also grills and steaks and chicken dishes. The vegetarian menu offers mushroom stroganoff fired and flamed in brandy and served with a mushroom sauce, Stilton and walnut pie, and a medley of deep-fried vegetables. There is also a full range of dessert dishes. On Sunday a set lunch is available. Meals are available from 12 noon to 2 pm and 7 pm to 10 pm on Monday to Friday, throughout opening hours on Saturday, and from 12 noon to 3 pm and 7 pm to 9 pm on Sunday.

The Abbey is part of the Pubmaster group and its traditional real ales are Worthington Best Bitter, Tetley Bitter and Bass. The two lagers served are Castlemaine XXXX and Carlsberg, with Dry Blackthorn cider and Murphy's Irish Stout also on tap. The hotel is open for drinking 'all day' from Monday to Saturday and from 12 noon to 3 pm and 7 pm to 10.30 pm on Sunday. There is a no-smoking section, a beer garden and a play area for children. Telephone: 01733 210200.

Three cornered bridge at Crowland.

How to get there: Crowland lies on the A1073, 9 miles south of Spalding and 7 miles north of Peterborough's ring road.

Parking: Ample parking space is available to the rear of the Abbey Hotel. There is good alternative parking just across the road, by the entrance to the abbey.

Length of the walk: 2 miles. OS map: Landranger 142 Peterborough and surrounding area (inn GR 241104).

Crowland is an ancient market town full of interest to any visitor, with the remains of the great Benedictine abbey and a unique triangular bridge built centuries ago by the crossroads in the town when these streets were still waterways. The historian Richard Gough once called this bridge 'the greatest curiosity in Britain if not in Europe'. The walk is an easy stroll on clear field paths and quiet back lanes – it certainly does not compare with the feat of Henry Girdlestone, a 56 year old Crowland man who walked 1,000 miles in 1,000 hours in 1844. A signboard recording his achievement can be found on the Spalding road just outside the town centre.

The Walk

Turn right out of the Abbey Hotel car park towards the abbey and right again at the abbey's entrance gate. Turn left along the churchyard wall and continue forward along the left-hand edge of the playing field and then down the path to the right, with a small dyke on your immediate right. Upon reaching the wooden footbridge and signpost go directly across the main road onto another signposted path and footbridge. Again there is a small dyke on the right of this path. Ignore the track on your left after some 300 yards and continue along the footpath until you reach the lane. Cross the stout footbridge with handrail and walk straight across the lane onto another signposted path. Follow this wide grass track, with a ditch on your left, for about 600 yards, then turn left over a waymarked footbridge to follow a good grass track between two arable fields. At the bend in the track over the wide drain continue forward, then turn left at the track T-junction, with a three-armed signpost and a tree belt on the right.

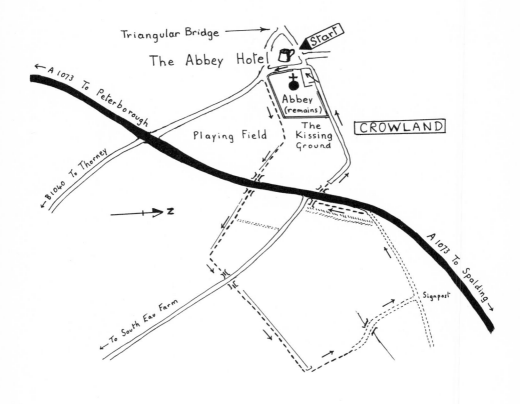

On reaching the main road again, keep on the signposted path to the left, with an embankment on your immediate left. After 200 yards cross the footbridge and then the main road to another footbridge and signpost directly opposite. This narrow path leads you along a back lane into the housing estate. Follow the road round to the left, passing the Kissing Ground and the abbey on your left, and go through the pedestrian gap in the car park wall and over the road, back to your starting place.

3 Tydd St Mary
The Tydd Gote Inn

Local wags will tell you that Tydd Gote really means 'Tide Go Out' although it is much more likely that the name derives from 'teat' – reflecting that the Tydds (there are more than one) stand on slightly higher ground. However, the tide does reach its limit up the river Nene a mile or so away and two great drains, the South Holland and the North Level, empty into the river nearby. Indeed, the Tydds could almost be on an island for they are bounded by water on three sides. Local names are fascinating – Foul Anchor, Four Gotes, Lady Nunn's Old Eau and Adventurers Lands all reflecting the history of the drainage of these fens.

In this far corner of Lincolnshire two other counties meet, Cambridgeshire and Norfolk. Within the Tydd Gote Inn, depending at which end of the lounge you happen to stand, you may either be in Lincolnshire or Cambridgeshire. This is an unspoilt and old-fashioned roadside pub without frills. On a summer evening it is very nice to sit out on the back terrace and watch a game of bowls on the pub's own well-kept bowling green. Everything is well-kept inside too, in an unpretentious way, with an open-plan bar and comfortable seating, a snug dining area with rectangular tables and bench seating and a games room offering a billiard table, a juke box and gaming machines. You will also find a beer garden, a family room and an outside play area for children. Overnight accommodation is available in five rooms, three of them en-suite. Children are welcome in the pub, but dogs should be left outside. Simple, good-value food is on offer, such as chilli con carne, steak and kidney pie, lasagne, jumbo sausage or beefburger with chips, half a chicken, and 'All Day Breakfast'. Rolls and sandwiches are available, also tea and coffee. Meals are served on Monday to Saturday from 12 noon to 3 pm and 6 pm to 9.30 pm, and on Sunday from 12 noon to 2 pm and 8 pm to 9.30 pm.

The Tydd Gote is a freehouse offering Elgood's Cambridge Bitter, as well as Mitchells and Butlers Mild, Worthington Best Bitter, Tennent's Extra, draught Guinness and Kilkenny Irish Beer. There are two ciders – Strongbow Dry and Woodpecker – and two lagers – Carlsberg and Carling Black Label. The inn is open from 11 am to 3 pm and 5.30 pm to 11 pm on Monday to Friday, all day (11 am to 11 pm) on Saturday, and 12 noon to 3 pm and 7 pm to 10.30 pm on Sunday.

Telephone: 01945 420653.

How to get there: The Tydd Gote lies on the A1101, 2½ miles from the Long Sutton roundabout on the A17(T), west of King's Lynn, and 6½ miles from Wisbech. If you approach from the north, the inn is on the left-hand side of the road, just before the large bridge over the North Level Main Drain.

Parking: Customers may park in the very adequate car park and the landlord does not mind walkers leaving cars there during their stroll. It is difficult, in this instance, to suggest a safe, alternative parking area off the main road.

Length of the walk: 1¾ miles. OS map: Landranger 131 Boston and Spalding area (inn GR 451178).

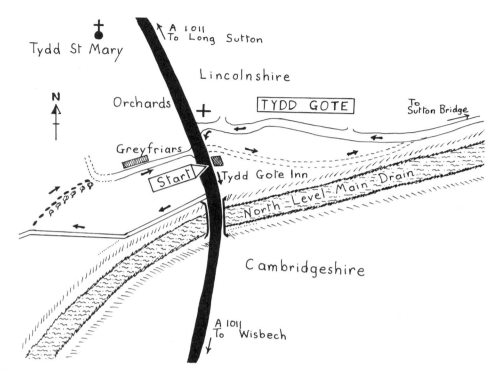

A good introduction to the fen and big sky country, this is an easy stroll, mostly on clear tracks or unfrequented lanes, along the broad North Level Main Drain and by the lovely old house of Greyfriars. The church of Tydd St Mary can be seen across the fields and it is said that Nicholas Breakspear (Adrian IV), the only Englishman ever to become Pope, was rector here in the 12th century.

The Walk
Turn left out of the inn car park for 150 yards. Just before the bridge, cross the road to take the little lane signposted 'Tydd St Giles', with the wide North Level Main Drain on your immediate left.

You can, if you wish, climb a stile and walk along the drain bank below the lane, to rejoin the lane where it turns sharply to the right by a double field gate and a notice forbidding cars along

North Level Main Drain.

the bank. After another 200 yards from the turn, where the lane bears to the left, take the pleasant grass path (signposted) on the right, following the line of old trees. Turn right on reaching the lane, with the lovely house and grounds of Greyfriars on your left. Greyfriars is a jumble of architectural styles and influences, with 17th and 18th-century elements and a 14th-century doorway in an adjoining wall that looks to have been imported from elsewhere.

Cross the main road and walk straight forward on a small lane, which becomes a track, with the Tydd Gote Inn over on your right. Pause to have a look at the boundary sign.

On reaching a lane turn left, back into the village, passing the post office and general store en route. When you reach the main road, turn left, back to your starting place.

Places of interest nearby
The *Butterfly and Falconry Park* at Long Sutton. Telephone: 01406 363833.

4 Witham on the Hill
The Six Bells

Witham on the Hill, once known as Witham-Super-Montem, in the rolling, limestone countryside of south Lincolnshire, is a small village set on a hill between the winding valleys of the East and West Glen rivers. The 'ham' in its name is a Danish legacy.

One Christmas Eve, in 1738, the bellringers left the church for the purpose of taking refreshment in the Black Dog, the village pub at that time, which was opposite the old tower. One ringer, with a greater thirst than the rest, insisted that they all should have another pitcher of ale before returning to their ringing. The extra mug saved their lives for, while they were drinking, the spire and part of the tower fell down. Unusually, the tower was rebuilt on the south side of the church, away from the nave. Also of interest is that the church has possessed a clock for over 400 years and this is one of the earliest examples of a clock in a church tower, dating back before the invention of the pendulum. Squire Fenwick from Witham Hall, a fine stone mansion in Queen Anne style built 200 years ago (now a boarding school), was responsible for moving the pub at the turn of the century. The Black Dog was situated opposite the gates of the Hall and the grooms from the Squire's stables were often to be found there – so he closed the pub and had the Six Bells built at the very end of the village.

The Six Bells is a handsome, stone-built inn, set in its own grounds in a splendid position, with picnic tables on the terrace at the front, and others in the pleasant garden at the side. There are three good rooms. One is a dining room (with a non-smoking section) able to seat 22 people. Another is a carpeted lounge bar with bench seating, a snug alcove, Ye Olde Wishing Wall with a notice informing guests that the management is not responsible for wishes that are not granted, and many mugs hanging on the ceiling. There is also a light, airy bar parlour with a quarry tiled floor and centre carpet, pool table, darts and a television. This is furnished with wooden rectangular tables, ladder-back chairs with cushions and bird pictures on the wall. The food on offer includes soup of the day served with a crusty baguette, garlic mushrooms, prawn cocktail and pâté with hot toast. Main courses range from steaks of various kinds, to roast chicken, deep fried scampi, home-made steak and ale pie, home-made lasagne, curry of the day, chilli con carne and Yorkshire pudding with various fillings. You will also find a children's menu, a range of hot and cold sweets and a traditional Sunday lunch. The pub is open for lunches on Monday to Sunday from 12 noon to 2 pm and for dinner on Saturday from 6.30 pm to 9 pm.

The inn is part of the Pubmaster group and the real ales served include Tetley Bitter, Whitbread Trophy and Bass. Guinness is available on draught and there are Stella Artois, Castlemaine XXXX and Carling Black Label lagers plus Dry Blackthorn cider. The opening times are from 12 noon to 3 pm every day, and from 6 pm to 11 pm on Monday to Saturday and 7 pm to 10.30 pm on Sunday. Dogs should be left outside the pub.

Telephone: 01778 590360.

How to get there: From Bourne take the A151 Corby Glen/Colsterworth road, westwards. After 1 mile take the left fork onto the A6121 Stamford road. Continue for almost 3 miles and turn right at the crossroads, signposted 'Witham on the Hill'. The Six Bells is on the right at the beginning of the village.

Parking: There is ample space at the side or the rear of the Six Bells. Avoid parking at the front if you intend leaving your car while doing the walk. Alternative parking may be available in the small car park by the church wall at the edge of the village green, unless it is Sunday.

Length of the walk: 2½ miles. OS map: Landranger 130 Grantham and surrounding area (inn GR 055163).

This is an easy walk through an attractive and interesting village and on, by good field paths, woodland and meadows, through gently undulating, landscape above the winding East Glen river. A glimpse of the 17th-century dovecote behind Palace Farm, ancient stocks for malefactors – the top rail of which was burnt on the bonfire to celebrate the Relief of Mafeking – and llamas may be seen en route.

The Walk

From the pub car park turn right into the village round the bends in the road to the church, passing Palace Farm. This was once the manor house, with village huts built around it. The name comes from it having been the former southern palace of the Bishops of Lincoln, conveniently situated a day's ride from the city. King John is said to have stayed there shortly before his death at Newark in October 1216. Palace Farm today is only one third of the original building, which was damaged by fire.

Near the church, note the Victorian schoolroom on the right, now the church hall, with its inscription: 'Train up a child in the way he should go and when he is old he will not part from it'. At the end of the church wall turn diagonally right across the village green, aiming for the telephone box. Walk down the steps to the stocks, now covered – to preserve them rather than to protect wrongdoers – and turn right off the road, with the little stream on your immediate right. The flow of the Bywell spring rarely fails even in drought conditions.

Having turned right up the lane, walk straight forward uphill on the signposted bridleway, with Hillcrest House on the left and later Nursery Plantation. After ½ mile on this track, turn right on a signposted bridleway by a metal field gate to walk along the edge of the tree belt for about 400 yards.

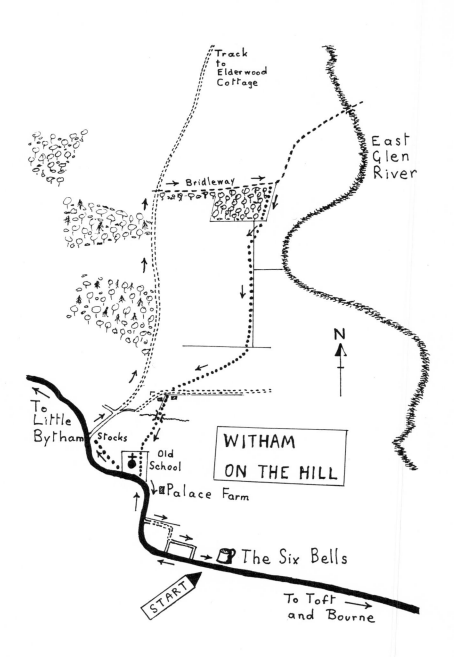

Track
to
Elderwood
Cottage

East
Glen
River

Bridleway

WITHAM

ON THE HILL

N

To
Little
Bytham

Stocks

Old
School

Palace Farm

The Six Bells

START

To Toft →
and Bourne

Where the bridleway turns left (waymark), turn right along the edge of the wood on an indistinct footpath for only about 200 yards. A stile has been promised at the fence by the wood edge and you turn diagonally right across the grass field to the end of the hedge on the right where there should be another new stile. Turn left along the field edge, with the hedge on your immediate left. At the end of this field, where you meet the line of electricity wires, again turn diagonally right across the field towards the house just to the right of the church spire. Turn right on meeting the wide track for a few yards and then left on a signposted path, with another house and garden on your right. Cross both stiles and the stout wooden footbridge and then walk straight forward, uphill, to a stile in the church wall. It may be possible to see llamas in the field on your left.

Do have a look in the church, with its list of vicars beginning with Walter de Driffield in 1200, 15 years before Magna Carta.

Turn left on leaving the church and follow the road round the right-hand bend. Directly opposite a farm entrance across the road, turn left on a concrete path and then follow the grass path by the line of trees on your left. Turn right at the garages and then left across the green to return to your starting place.

Places of interest nearby
Impressive *Grimsthorpe Castle*, north-west of Bourne, is set in spectacular parkland. There are gardens and a nature trail. Telephone: 01778 591205. On Fridays there are guided tours around the *Lincolnshire Steam Beer Co.*, The Maltings Brewery, St Peter's Road, Bourne. Telephone: 01778 394422.

5 Skillington
The Blue Horse Inn

Whoever saw a blue horse? Sir William Manners offered free ale on his properties to every tenant who promised to support the Whig candidate and the inn signs were painted blue as an extra election gimmick. At one time there was a number of other 'blue' pubs in the neighbourhood, including the Blue Dog, the Blue Fox, the Blue Cow and the Blue Bull.

Skillington has a pleasant village green, dominated by an imposing stone-built Wesleyan Methodist chapel, and two pubs, one of which is the Blue Horse Inn and Restaurant, a freehouse that genuinely reflects traditional village life and work, with an old horse-plough hoisted on the wall outside to emphasise the connection. There is another smaller green in the village and this one has the base of an old market cross on it. Above the green is the parish church of St James with 1,000 years of history and a listing in the Domesday Book. Inside there is some interesting information and a memorial window relating to the tragic death of the Rev Charles Hudson on the Matterhorn in 1866. As a child

Isaac Newton attended the dame school once held in the church.

The Blue Horse's comfortable, stone-built lounge bar, with its old beams, brass-topped tables and settles round the wall, epitomises what a village inn should be. The lounge is L-shaped with a good open fire in season to add to the welcome. The restaurant is an attractive room capable of seating 52 people. The range and quality of the food on offer both here and from the bar is a further pleasant surprise. It includes fillet of duck with orange sauce and salad, 'Salmon Balmoral' with asparagus tips in a lobster sauce and 'Chicken Cotswold', breast of chicken topped with Stilton cheese. There is also quite a list of vegetarian dishes, including 'Caribbean Vegetarian Wellington', a mixture of vegetables and tropical fruits. Traditional Sunday lunches are served and from Monday to Saturday a senior citizens' special lunch is available at a very modest price. It would be wise to book in advance for the restaurant, especially at weekends. Drinks include Tetley Bitter, Ind Coope Burton Ale, Ansells Bitter and Kilkenny Irish Beer. Draught Guinness and two Carlsberg lagers are on offer and, unusually, there are chilled wines on tap. The inn and restaurant are open from 11 am to 3 pm on Monday to Saturday and from 12 noon to 4 pm on Sunday. Throughout the week evening opening is between 7 pm and 11 pm. Food is available from 12 noon to 2 pm and from 7 pm to 10 pm throughout the week.

Telephone: 01476 860423.

How to get there: Turn westwards off the A1 at the Colsterworth roundabout, between Grantham and Stamford. Go along the B676 for almost 2 miles to the Stainby crossroads, then turn northwards to Skillington. The village green and the inn are on your left as you enter the village.

Parking: There is a small inn car park but should this be full park at the top of the village green near to the Methodist chapel.

Length of the walk: 2 miles. OS map: Landranger 130 Grantham and surrounding area (inn GR 898257).

This is a peaceful and interesting walk along an ancient track and through the secluded valley of the Cringle Brook. In

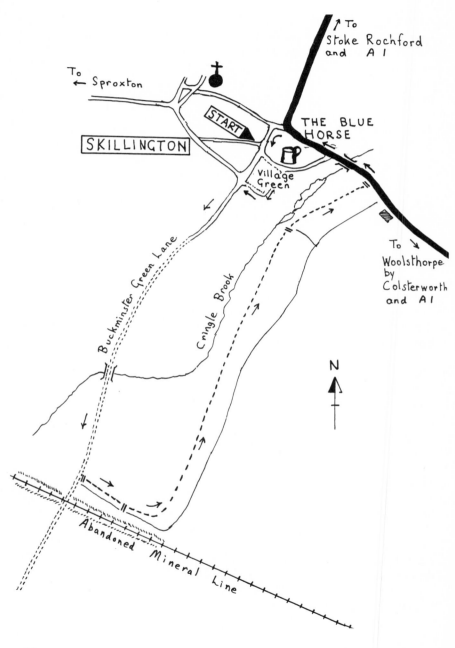

summertime the grassland, at present under the Countryside Commission Stewardship Scheme, a government-funded conservation agreement, is rich in flowers, especially around the little lake, and these attract butterflies and other insects. Hedges provide colour and interest throughout the year, as well as feeding and nesting sites for many species of birds.

The Walk

Turn left out of the inn and walk across the green to the Methodist chapel. Then turn left up the lane, with the chapel on your immediate left. The lane soon becomes a track and continues forward down into the dip to cross the Cringle Brook.

Some 350 yards up the slope beyond Cringle Brook bridge turn left at the stile and Stewardship notice, which explains about access and provides a map. Proceed straight across the field to a second stile, with the embankment of the old railway line over on the right. Cross this second stile and turn diagonally left down the valley.

There is no need to stay with a public right of way on this Stewardship land, but it is probably better underfoot to keep to the higher slope on the right-hand side of the valley. Towards the bottom of the valley there is another stile and then a footbridge. Avoid the marsh and keep to the higher ground, with the lake on your left below. You can see the lane in front and some 50 yards to the right of the road bridge you will discover a stile in the roadside hedge and another Stewardship notice.

Cross the stile and turn left down the lane, back into the village. After 500 yards turn left by the Cross Swords public house and just beyond is the village green and your starting place.

Places of interest nearby

The National Trust's *Woolsthorpe Manor*, a small 17th-century farmhouse (GR 923246) at Woolsthorpe by Colsterworth, about 2½ miles from Skillington, was the birthplace and family home of Sir Isaac Newton. Some of his major work was formulated here during the Plague years of 1665–66. The orchard includes a descendant of the famous apple tree. It is open from 1 April until the end of October, Wednesday to Sunday inclusive and bank holiday Monday. Telephone: 01476 860338.

Skillington.

Woolsthorpe by Belvoir
The Rutland Arms/The Dirty Duck

Woolsthorpe is only just in Lincolnshire, for the Leicestershire border is literally yards away while the Nottinghamshire border lies some 4 miles to the north-west. Beware though, for there are two Woolsthorpes in Lincolnshire, not many miles apart. The other Woolsthorpe (by Colsterworth) was the home of Sir Isaac Newton. Our Woolsthorpe is situated beside the Grantham canal and within sight of Belvoir Castle, the seat of the Duke of Rutland. The Rutland Arms is widely known as the Dirty Duck and when you examine the wind vane a little more closely you may understand the reason.

The Dirty Duck is around 270 years old and was originally a smallholding and an alehouse long before the canal was built. Nowadays, despite the lack of canal traffic, it is a very popular watering hole for locals, walkers along the Viking Way, anglers, caravanners and visitors looking for the other Woolsthorpe. The landlord boasts that the pub is in one of the most beautiful settings in the whole area. It has a long, comfortably furnished lounge bar

Restored locks on the Grantham canal.

with a good view of Belvoir Castle from the end windows, a bar with an adjoining games room and pool table, a family room and a superb function room. A no-smoking section is available. There are picnic tables on the front patio, a children's play area with climbing frame and swings, and well-behaved dogs are welcome. While the pub does not offer overnight accommodation, it is possible to bring a tent or caravan and to camp within the extensive grounds.

The snack menu ranges from beefburgers, veggieburgers, cold ham and eggs, baked potatoes with various fillings and several differently filled baps. Vegetarians can choose home-made nut roast with a mushroom sauce or cannelloni with spinach and ricotta cheese. There is a wide selection of sweets for dessert. The food on offer changes with the seasons and a blackboard menu shows the current dishes. Meals are served from 12 noon to 3 pm and 7 pm to 10 pm every day, with a 6.30 pm start on Monday to Saturday in summertime. This is a freehouse and the well-kept beers on handpump include Flowers Original, Boddingtons Bitter, Castle Eden Ale and three lagers, Whitbread Gold Label, Stella Artois and Heineken. The three ciders are Scrumpy Jack, Woodpecker and Strongbow Medium Dry. There is also draught

Guinness and a wide range of wines. The inn is open from 11 am (12 noon on Sunday) to 3 pm and 7 pm to 11 pm (10.30 pm on Sunday).
Telephone: 01476 870360.

How to get there: From the A1 at Grantham take the A607 Melton Mowbray road. After 2½ miles turn right at Denton crossroads and then left in Denton village for another 2½ miles to Woolsthorpe by Belvoir. Turn right at the crossroads in the village for ½ mile and the Dirty Duck is signposted on the right.

Parking: There is ample parking at all times and the landlord has no objection to anyone leaving a car there while they are on the walk.

Length of the walk: 2½ miles. OS map: Landranger 130 Grantham and surrounding area (inn GR 811351).

A gentle walk of contrasts over level ground, with a flight of locks on the canal, hump-backed bridges, a bit of the Viking Way long-distance recreational path and a short section of Sewstern Lane, a prehistoric, unsurfaced route far older than the parallel Roman road that became the Great North Road and then the A1.

The Walk

Turn right out of the car park by the edge of the canal for 20 yards and then go up the steps to the bridge. Cross the bridge and turn right to the Willis Locks. Follow the towpath round the bend for about 500 yards to the little hump-backed bridge. Climb onto the pathway of the unsurfaced Longmoor Lane and walk forward for ¾ mile. Upon reaching the tree-lined road with its wide grass verges, turn left. At the bend in the road turn left by the memorial ladder stile onto Sewstern Lane. The field gate, once locked, is now missing so the elegant stile has become unnecessary.

On reaching a wooden field gate across Sewstern Lane, turn right down to the canal lock and weir and then left along the canal bank on the wide, green trackway, with the canal on your immediate right. On reaching the bridge by the Willis Locks turn right, back to the Dirty Duck.

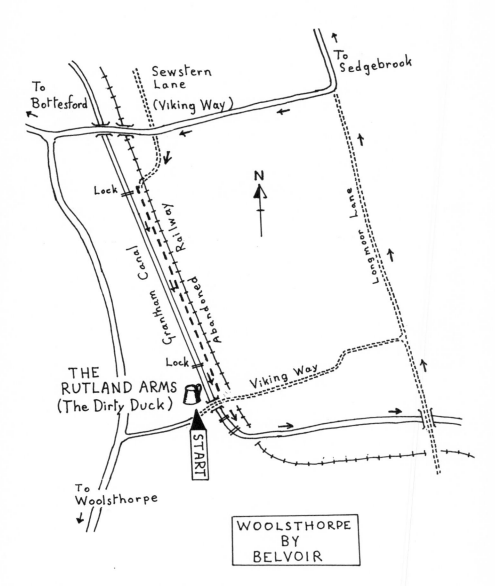

To Bottesford

Sewstern Lane (Viking Way)

To Sedgebrook

N

Lock

Grantham Canal

Abandoned Railway

Longmoor Lane

Lock

Viking Way

THE RUTLAND ARMS (The Dirty Duck)

START

To Woolsthorpe

WOOLSTHORPE BY BELVOIR

Places of interest nearby

Belvoir Castle is open for visitors from 1 April until 30 September, between 11 am and 5 pm. Medieval jousting tournaments and siege re-enactments are a popular feature. Telephone: 01476 870262.

7 Langrick Bridge
The Ferry Boat

Langrick ('long reach'), in Holland Fen, refers to the ebb of tide for the sea reached this far up the Witham before the erection of Boston Sluice. Like so many of Lincolnshire's fen parishes, Langrick is new. When the land was finally drained and enclosed in 1802 it had 'neither house nor inhabitant', and now it consists of two small groups of houses at Langrick and Langrick Bridge plus scattered farms. The old chain ferry disappeared with the construction of the steel bridge over the river in 1909 and it is only remembered today by the name of the inn and its attractive sign. The good fishing offered by the Witham meant that Langrick once hosted the National Angling Championships.

Today the Ferry Boat is a neat, civilised and friendly fenland pub with white external walls and interior low beams decorated by a variety of horse brasses. It has an attractive lounge plus a snug bar with bench seats and rectangular tables and old prints on the walls. Two bay windows overlook a small garden. The red-tiled floor of the bar parlour is quite a contrast. There is bench seating

Hedgehog Bridge.

here too, and plates along a rail, a juke box, a dartboard and a pool table. The pub was once used as a goose shoeing station, where the birds were driven through hot tar to prepare their feet for the long walk to the London markets. Brothertoft, to the south, was a centre of the trade and was formerly known as Goosetoft.

There is a wide choice of food, including the delicious Ferry mixed grill, steaks, pork chops, chicken in various forms, fish dishes, spaghetti bolognaise, home-made steak and kidney pie and chilli and rice pie, ham and eggs, vegetable lasagne and salads. Among the sweets are Mississippi mud pie, banoffee pie, 'Tropical Paradise', home-made apple pie with cream and knickerbocker glory. Tea and coffee are also available. During the week, meals are served from 11.30 am to 2.30 pm and on Tuesday, Wednesday and Friday evenings from 7.30 pm to 10.30 pm. There is no food at lunchtime on Saturday but the evening times are 7 pm to 10.30 pm. On Sunday you can eat between 12 noon and 2 pm and in the evening from 7 pm to 10.30 pm. The pub is a freehouse serving Home Mild and Bitter, Younger Best Bitter, draught Guinness, McEwan's lager and Woodpecker cider. It is a favourite local for many of the workers in the intensively-farmed

land in the immediate area and for fishermen during the season. Dogs are welcome in the bar parlour. The opening times on Monday to Saturday are from 11 am to 2.30 pm and 6.30 pm (7 pm on Saturday) to 11 pm, and on Sunday from 12 noon to 3 pm and 7 pm to 10.30 pm.
Telephone: 01205 280273.

How to get there: Langrick Bridge lies 2½ miles off the A1121 Boston to Sleaford road. Go north at the Hubbert's Bridge crossing onto the B1192 Horncastle road. Just after the bridge over the river Witham, the pub is on the right.

Parking: There is an adequate car park at the side of the pub and the landlady is quite willing for walkers to leave their cars. There isn't any other suitable place in the immediate vicinity.

Length of the walk: 3 miles. OS map: 131 Boston and Spalding area (inn GR 266476).

This walk is a good introduction to the Lincolnshire fen with its wide horizons, fertile fields and enormous, long, straight drains. It is big sky country indeed. The route takes you beside the North Forty Foot Drain to Brothertoft, with views of Boston Stump. Some stump!

The Walk
Turn left out of the pub car park to cross the bridge over the river Witham by the footway. Go over the road and turn right down the side lane, signposted 'Holland Fen', for about 350 yards. Where the lane turns right leave it to follow the good, stoned track with a footpath signpost, on your left.

At the left-hand bend in the track cross the wooden footbridge and continue straight forward on a clear path at the field edge, with a dyke on your immediate left. At the Hedgehog Bridge Farm garden there is a waymark and here you leave the driveway to turn right through the farm buildings (waymark) on the right and on to the road, by the footpath signpost near the red telephone kiosk.

Turn left along the road, with the Forty Foot Drain and the curious little footbridge on your right, with perhaps a swan

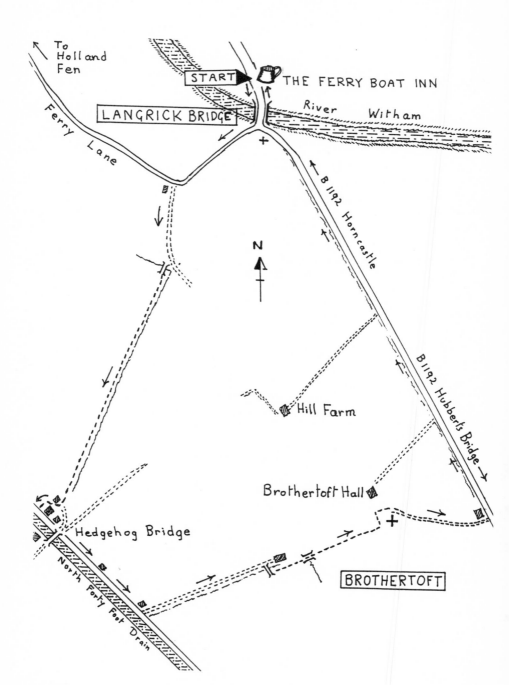

To Holland Fen

START THE FERRY BOAT INN

LANGRICK BRIDGE

River Witham

Ferry Lane

B 1192 Horncastle

N

B 1192 Hubberts Bridge

Hill Farm

Brothertoft Hall

Hedgehog Bridge

BROTHERTOFT

North Forty Foot Drain

38

nesting just beyond the bridge. The white residence on your left was originally the Old Plough Inn and a small plaque on the wall denotes this. Some 500 yards beyond Hedgehog Bridge, by a house on the left, turn left on a signposted path along a good track leading towards Brothertoft church. Cross the broad dyke on the right on the new waymarked footbridge and turn immediately left down the field edge to the church, with an abandoned cottage and farmyard on your left across the dyke. Cross the splendid new footbridge with handrails and continue forward to the church. Turn left through the iron handgate into the churchyard and then right to cross with care the widely-spaced cattle grid. Turn right down the gravelled drive to the road.

Cross the second cattle grid (again with care) and go over the road to turn left towards Langrick Bridge, keeping on the wide grass verge, with Brothertoft village hall on your left. On reaching the bridge cross over the river Witham, back to your starting place.

Places of interest nearby

St Botolph's church, Boston (Boston Stump) with its magnificent tower, over 260 ft above the ground, and warning bell. The tower is open daily, except Sunday and Christmas Day. Telephone: 01205 362864. At the *Maud Foster Windmill*, just to the north-east of Boston town centre, visitors may climb all seven floors and view the milling process in action. Telephone: 01205 352188. North of Boston, the *Sibsey Trader Mill* is open on occasional milling days. Telephone: 01604 730320.

8 Folkingham
The Greyhound Inn

The Greyhound is a fabulous refurbished coaching inn on the old London Road halfway between Bourne and Sleaford. Situated at the head of the wide main street in this interesting village, it was once the boarding point for the London coach. As early as 1611 there was a mention of 'an ale-house a'top Market Place in Folkingham'. In 1788 a court house and assembly room were added and the cells, once used by prisoners, have become the beer cellar of today. After sentencing, lucky prisoners were taken across the road to the House of Correction but the less fortunate were taken by waggon to Boston for transportation to the Colonies. Beer brewed on the premises was fourpence a gallon in 1788, a bottle of sherry cost four shillings and sixpence and a meal three shillings and threepence.

Now the Greyhound is a freehouse serving Courage Best Bitter, Courage Directors and John Smith's Bitter. Lagers include Foster's, Kronenburg 1664 and Miller Pilsner. Scrumpy Jack is on draught and there is also Woodpecker cider. The stout on offer is Beamish. A delightful atrium coffee lounge has been constructed in the old coaching entrance and you will also find a wine bar serving a full wine list, a restaurant, a patio with tables, a family room, a no-smoking area and a beer garden. Overnight accommodation is available. The bar is open on Monday to Saturday from 11 am to 3 pm and 5.30 pm to 11 pm, and on Sunday from 12 noon to 2 pm and 7 pm to 10.30 pm. Dogs should be left outside.

The wide choice of bar food includes sandwiches of various kinds, jacket potatoes, ploughman's and a range of omelettes – ham, mushroom, cheese and onion or prawn. Meals include soup of the day, prawn platter, garlic mushrooms, crunchy garlic bread, crumbed Brie wedges or mussels in white wine sauce. Roast pheasant with bacon, mushroom and gravy, spicy beef, steak and ale pie, breast of duck, plaice served with white wine, mushroom stroganoff and saffron rice or a vegetable risotto are other examples of the main meals on offer. The range of sweets is just as varied and exciting. Food is served on Monday to Saturday from 11 am to 2.30 pm and 5.30 pm to 10 pm, and on Sunday from 12 noon to 3 pm and 7 pm to 10 pm.

Telephone: 01529 497497.

The House of Correction, Folkingham.

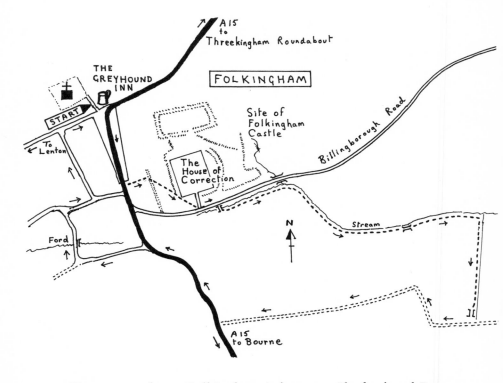

How to get there: Folkingham is between Sleaford and Bourne on the A15 road, some 9 miles from either town. The Greyhound Inn dominates the main street.

Parking: There is free parking in the wide market place immediately in front of the Greyhound Inn, plus an adequate car park behind the inn.

Length of the walk: 2 miles. OS map: 130 Grantham and surrounding area (inn GR 071334).

This absorbing short walk circles much of a village that was once of some importance, taking you past the strange House of Correction, near to the castle site and then by a stream along a small valley and over a largely undiscovered ford behind the wide main street.

The Walk

Leave the inn car park to walk straight down the spacious market place for 300 yards. Turn left on a waymarked path, with a garage on your immediate right. By the waymark, cross the track to the stile and then proceed diagonally right across the grass field to the moat bordering the House of Correction. Follow the path round to the right to the end of the wall where there is a signpost and stile on the lane. Cross the stile and turn left for a few yards and then right to join the signposted path at the side of the Anglian Water Pumping Station.

Cross the concrete bridge and turn immediately left to take a diverted public footpath that now follows the stream edge near the road. Over to the left is the site of the Norman castle, which was rebuilt in the 14th century but later destroyed by Cromwell's forces in the Civil War. Only the grassy mound remains today, with remnants of the moat. The House of Correction was built in 1825 on the ruins of the inner bailey of the castle. In 1987 the Landmark Trust converted the remains of the original building.

Continue along the edge of the water and cross a wooden footbridge. At the end of the first field beyond the bridge turn right (waymark) uphill, with a ditch on the left, to the signpost on the skyline and another small footbridge. Turn right on this 'road used as a public path' to the main road and right again at the road, towards the village. Just beyond the bend cross the road to turn left up Greenfields Lane. Turn right at the track junction down to the ford with a side bridge. Turn right again at Low Farm entrance down Spring Lane and left up Chapel Lane, the first lane on your left. At the T-junction turn right down to Folkingham church and your starting place.

Take time, if you can, to explore St Andrew's with its 15th-century tower. This big church has been well restored and is worthy of a much larger place. Inside you will see stocks and a whipping post. Scots prisoners and supporters of James II were kept in the church after the battle of Swatow Common in 1689. There is a very fine chestnut tree shading the churchyard gate, reputed to be 14 ft round the trunk.

9 Scopwick
The Royal Oak

The Royal Oak sign depicts Charles II escaping after the battle of Worcester in 1651. He was helped by the Pendrel brothers in Shropshire who dressed him in woodman's clothing and darkened his face with soot. Pubs named the Black Boy are also recalling the disguised king. Charles II spent a day and a night hidden in the branches of a huge oak tree and on his return to power he gave the Pendrel family a pension that their descendants receive to this day.

Scopwick which comes from the Old English scaep-wick meaning sheep farm, is on heathland just above Kesteven Fen. This strip of land about three miles wide runs down the eastern side of Kesteven all the way from Lincoln to Market Deeping. Grey walls, red roofs and a stream running through the village at right angles to the main road, with the Royal Oak at the junction, make an attractive setting. The pub has a traditionally furnished L-shaped bar with a dining alcove in one part of the L and an open fire in season. The pride and joy of the landlord is a high-tech jukebox offering some 100 CDs with up to 20 tunes on each. There is a pool table and a television in this part of the bar, with settles around the wall. A separate dining room is open at lunchtime on Sunday (when a traditional roast is on offer), and every evening. There are picnic tables at the front of the pub by the stream.

The pub serves John Smith's Bitter, Tetley Bitter, draught Guinness, Foster's and Carlsberg lager, Gaymer's Old English strong and Strongbow Dry cider. Bar food includes home-made soup, prawn cocktail and smoked mackerel as starters, and main course dishes such as steaks cooked to your liking, served with chips, peas and salad garnish, salads, Irish stew with onions and mushrooms cooked in Guinness, omelettes and ploughman's. Among the home-made sweets are treacle pudding and custard, apple and raspberry charlotte with custard, orange and Cointreau gateau and pancakes with Bailey's Irish Cream. Sandwiches are made to order and there is a blackboard menu giving the dish of the day. Bar meals are served at lunchtime on Monday to Saturday (11.30 am to 2 pm) and in the evening on Monday to Thursday (7 pm to 9 pm). The pub's opening hours on Monday to Saturday are from 11 am to 3 pm and 7 pm to 11 pm, and on Sunday from 12 noon to 3 pm and 7 pm to 10.30 pm.
Telephone: 01526 320285.

How to get there: Scopwick is on the B1188 Lincoln to Sleaford road, 10 miles from Lincoln or 7 miles from Sleaford.

Parking: There is ample car parking either in front of the pub or in the alternative car park at the rear.

Length of the walk: 2½ miles. OS map: Landranger 121 Lincoln and surrounding area (inn GR 068580).

A pleasant, well-waymarked walk along green lanes and clear public footpaths, with some unexpected sculpture en route. Part of the walk is over a network of North Kesteven District Council's 'Stepping Out' recreational routes. For a short distance the walk follows the stream, with its considerable duck population enlivening your progress.

Sculpture on Trundle Lane.

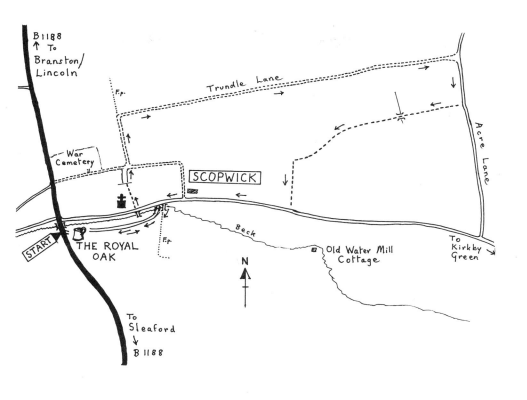

The Walk

Turn right out of the pub down Brookside, with the stream on your left, for 250 yards and then go left over the beck across the clapper bridge and over the road to the church. Follow the concrete path at the side of the church wall by a sign 'To the war graves' and continue straight forward through the small bungalow complex.

The war graves are on your left when you reach the green lane, but turn right for only a few yards and then left up a broad green lane which is a 'road used as a public path' (RUPP) named Trundle Lane.

Turn right by the stile to remain on the broad green lane which is up to 60 ft wide in places, pausing en route to examine the wood sculpture on the right. *The Seated Woman* was carved by

47

Rosie Bradshaw in 1991, and represents a dryad or tree spirit. The figure is 7 ft tall and is carved from a single piece of elm. At the junction with Acre Lane turn right up this good track for 300 yards and then right again on a waymarked footpath, with a hedge on your left. Cross the sturdy footbridge and continue forward on the waymarked path. Bear left to the road on reaching the horse paddock.

Turn right along Main Street, but after 500 yards cross the road and the small footbridge by the footpath sign and then the larger bridge over the beck. Turn right along Brookside, with the beck now on your right, to return to your starting place.

Places of interest nearby
North Ings Farm Museum at Dorrington, to the south, displays agricultural machinery and vintage tractors. It also has a working narrow gauge railway. Telephone: 01526 833100. *Timberland Pumping Station* and *Tales of the Riverbank*, located on the minor road alongside the river Witham between Tattershall Bridge and Kirkstead Bridge, give a fascinating history of fen drainage. Admission free. *Timberland Art and Design Craft Workshop* in Church Lane, Timberland. Telephone: 01526 378222.

10 Candlesby
The Royal Oak

Yet another Royal Oak! After his defeat at the battle of Worcester in 1651 Charles II, along with his aide Colonel Carter, hid in the Boscobel Oak near Shifnal, Shropshire, in order to escape from pursuing Roundhead soldiers. On his return to the throne, the King's birthday, May 29th, was celebrated as Royal Oak Day as a thanksgiving. The popularity of the sign may be attributed to general rejoicing that the monarchy had been restored.

Candlesby is a pleasant little village near the foot of the wolds. The yellow brick church of St Benedict stands among the trees as does Candlesby Hall, a charming 18th-century house overlooking a large park. This inn, a typical brick-built village house with a white-painted gable end has a tasteful modern extension that blends in extremely well with the original building. There are shrubs and flower boxes and a very original ostrich and a crocodile made entirely out of spare parts of farm machinery that are well worth photographing as curiosities. There is a beer garden and, indoors, you will find a bar parlour with billiards and darts, a family room and a no-smoking area. The carpeted lounge bar has an attractive dining room alcove and the very pleasant new extension is a light, airy room with a polished quarry-tiled floor. Pictures of the locality and of aircraft are on display and for sale. One double room is available for overnight accommodation. Dogs are only permitted in the garden, on a lead.

It is not often that the trout offered in a pub have actually been caught by the landlord but this certainly happens at the Royal Oak. Examples of bar snacks are salads with honey-roasted ham, freshly made sandwiches to order and ploughman's. Starter courses include herring in a sweet dill sauce, Scottish salmon, prawn cocktail and smoked mackerel with horseradish cream. Among the main courses are fillet of pork cooked in cider and cream, honey-roasted duck, pheasant and gammon. Royal Oak puddings range from treacle tart, summer pudding, sticky toffee pudding with pecan sauce and chocolate truffle tart to fresh fruit flan. Meals are available from 12 noon to 2 pm and 7 pm to 9.30 pm between Tuesday evening and Sunday lunchtime. Booking for meals is advisable.

The Royal Oak is a freehouse serving Bateman Best Bitter, Mansfield Bitter, Adnams Southwold Bitter and Foster's Australian Beer. Draught Guinness, Scrumpy Jack cider and Carlsberg Export lager are also available. The pub is closed on Sunday evening, all day Monday and at Tuesday lunchtime, but at other times the hours are from 12 noon to 3 pm and 7 pm to 11 pm.

Telephone: 01754 890259.

How to get there: Driving towards Skegness on the A1028 road, turn off right down the lane to Candlesby, just beyond the prominent communications mast, or from the Gunby roundabout take the A158 Partney road westwards for almost a mile. The Royal Oak is situated on the crossroads in the village.

Parking: There is a good gravelled car park at the Royal Oak entrance by the 'ostrich' or, alternatively, across the road in front of the pub. Limited roadside parking could be possible elsewhere in the village with care.

Length of the walk: 2½ miles. OS map: Landranger 122 Skegness area (inn GR 455676).

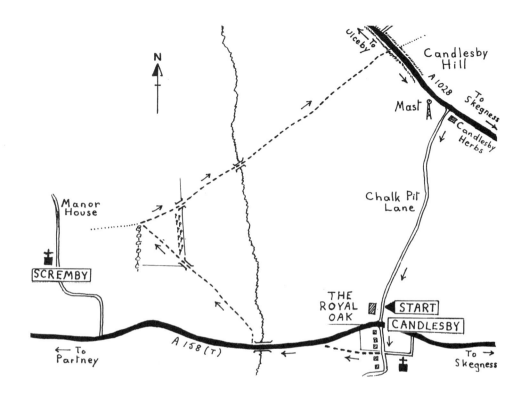

This leisurely short walk takes you on footpaths away from the village towards Scremby Manor and then up the gentle slope of the extreme edge of the Wolds escarpment. You are not far from the sea here and from Chalk Pit Lane by Candlesby Herbs, given the right weather conditions, it is often possible to see Boston Stump on the Lincolnshire coast and Norfolk across the Wash.

The Walk

On leaving the pub walk down to the crossroads and go straight across the main road towards the church. After 150 yards and directly opposite the lane on the left turn right through the iron handgate into the garden of a house. A promise to erect a footpath sign here has been made. Walk up the garden, with the house on the left, to a stile. In the arable field continue forward, with the

Ostrich made out of old farm machinery.

hedge on your immediate right, and keep the same line to the road after leaving the hedge. There is a signpost and stile at the roadside.

Turn left along the road for 150 yards and cross it by the bridge over the stream. There is a signpost and stile here and you follow the direction diagonally left across the field to a concrete footbridge with a prominent guidance post. In the next field continue on the same line to the right-hand edge of the line of trees and bushes. Here you join the path leading to Scremby Manor, but turn right to follow the waymarked path down into the valley, going over two footbridges en route. After crossing the second bridge at the stream walk uphill between the crop boundaries to a signpost and roughly cut steps leading up the embankment to the main road. Turn right on the road, towards the communications mast, and right again by Candlesby Herbs to walk downhill, back to your starting point.

Places of interest nearby
Candlesby Herbs welcomes callers and it is an interesting place to visit. Open daily (except Monday). Telephone: 01754 890211. *Gunby Hall*, a National Trust property, is a mile away in the next village. The house and grounds are open from 1 April to the end of September. Gunby, with its outstanding walled garden, is the house Tennyson is said to have had in mind when he wrote:

> 'Softer than sleep – all things in order stood
> A haunt of ancient peace.'

Some 3 miles from Candlesby crossroads, along a winding back lane, is *Northcote Heavy Horse Centre*, Great Steeping. Telephone: 01754 830286.

11 Aubourn
The Royal Oak

Aubourn, derived from the early Anglian place-name 'Alder-burn' in the 7th or 8th century, is called after the trees growing along the riverside. Settlements beside the river meant fresh drinking water, for people and livestock, wet meadowland for grass and hay, food to catch and plenty of waterside timber for building. The village today rests quietly on a back road where a jay-walking mallard could well hold up the cars despite the one-way traffic system.

Spotless and warmly welcoming, the Royal Oak is a freehouse with a well-earned local reputation for hospitality. It serves Bateman XB and XXXB and Sam Smith Old Brewery plus two regularly changing guest ales, two draught ciders, Strongbow and Woodpecker, and draught Guinness. There is also a cellar with a selection of good wine. The bar motto 'There are no strangers here, Only friends we have not yet met' is a realistic portrayal of the attitude of the landlord and staff to their customers. It is an interesting pub, full of rambling corners, with comfortable settees, low beams, horse brasses and prints on the walls. There are bench seats with floral covers, stout rectangular tables and a games section in one room. Outside, you will find two patio areas with picnic tables – one at the front and the other at the back, overlooking the popular children's play area, which is in a sheltered paddock. Children are permitted in the function room at lunchtimes and until 8.30 pm in the evenings.

As for food, the menus change with the seasons and all meals are fresh to order. A typical summertime menu might include something like tagliatelle topped with a sauce containing chunks of smoked haddock, prawns and mushrooms, served in an individual dish with French fries and salad, or vegetable lasagne. Salads and ploughman's are usually available. Examples of the delectable desserts are 'Nuts about chocolate and cream' and Dutch apricot crumble flan. The pub is open from 12 noon to 2.30 pm and 7 pm to 11 pm (10.30 pm on Sunday), with last orders for meals at 2 pm (1.45 pm on Sunday) and 9.45 pm.

Telephone: 01522 788291.

How to get there: Aubourn is some 2 miles off the main A46(T) road between Lincoln and Newark. If travelling towards Newark, the Haddington/Aubourn turn off is the first road on the left after the Lincoln bypass roundabout on the old Foss Way. Aubourn is signposted at Haddington crossroads. The Royal Oak is on the left as you enter the village on the one-way road system.

Parking: There is ample space at the Royal Oak, but please park away from the main entrance. As an alternative, you may be able to park on Blackmoor Road by the church entrance path.

Length of the walk: 2¼ miles. OS map: Landranger 121 Lincoln and surrounding area (inn GR 925628).

An easy walk in the flat land below the long line of the escarpment edge known locally as the Cliff, with distant views of Lincoln's cathedral set high upon the hill. You may disturb a heron patrolling the sluggish waters of the Witham in a leisurely manner – or some of the many ducks. You cross the river by a 'bridleway' bridge that would need a very acrobatic horse indeed to negotiate the walkway. The Hall, whose driveway you use to return to the village, has been occupied by the Neville family for over three and a half centuries.

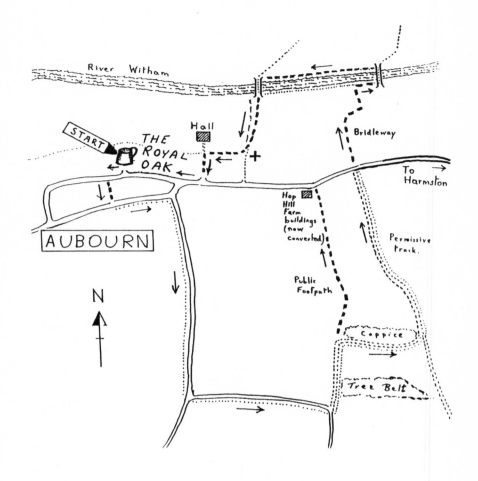

The Walk

Turn right out of the car park for 150 yards and then go left up the alleyway directly opposite the brick bus shelter. On reaching the lane turn left for 200 yards and then right at the T-junction onto the metalled track marked 'Public Way to Bassingham'. Turn left along the metalled track marked 'Marlborough Farm' instead of proceeding straight forward to Bassingham. Leave the track after 500 yards, where it turns sharply right, and proceed to the left on the waymarked public right of way over a good stoned track with a tree belt on the right.

Where this track turns right it becomes a permissive path and you may use either route. The clearly-defined public footpath continues diagonally left across the arable field to Hop Hill Farm buildings, where there is a wooden footpath signpost and a stile. Turn right on Blackmoor Road to join up with the permissive route. If using the permissive path, continue, with the mixed coppice on your immediate left, and at the track junction and hard standing turn left up to Blackmoor Road.

Cross the road directly onto the signposted bridleway but climb the stile at the side of the wooden field gate to walk along the top of the new floodbank, for the bridleway proper is frequently churned up and sometimes under water. Turn right along the river bank for a few yards to the high level metal bridge over the river Witham. How any horse could cross this supposedly bridleway bridge is difficult to imagine. After going over the river turn left along the bank to the concrete bridge. Climb the step stile on the right and walk forward towards the church, with the hedge and Hall lake on your right. Go through the kissing-gate into the churchyard and, after looking at the church, walk down to the waymarked gate leading into the Hall grounds. Go past the estate office and turn left down the main drive until you reach the road. Turn right at the road, back to your starting place.

Places of interest nearby
Aubourn Hall gardens are open to visitors on Wednesdays in July and August, between 2 pm and 6 pm. The admission charges are donated to local charities. Telephone: 01522 788270.

12 Stow in Lindsey
The Cross Keys

Cross Keys are a common sign in Christian heraldry and refer to St Peter, to whom Jesus said: 'I will give unto thee the keys to the kingdom of Heaven'. The papal arms show cross keys and they occur again in the arms of various bishops, particularly where the cathedral is dedicated to St Peter.

The earliest church at Stow was built by King Efrid in AD 678 and it was said to have been the Saxon cathedral of the diocese of Lindsey. This church was burnt down by marauding Vikings who wintered at Torksey on the Trent, only a few miles away. It was rebuilt between 1034 and 1050 when it was enriched and endowed by Leofric, Earl of Mercia, and his well-known wife, Lady Godiva. Regius became its first Norman bishop after the Conquest and he later moved his see from Stow into Lincoln. A quiet village, lying a mile from the Roman Tillbridge Lane, which links Ermine Street with a Trent river crossing, Stow in Lindsey is said to be the site of the Roman station of Sidnacester. The church is something to marvel at, having the most sumptuous

Norman parochial chancel in England, and there is a village green with a whipping post, and long views up to the western ridge of the Wolds, known locally as the Cliff, that sweep from the Humber right across Lincolnshire and down to the Cotswolds. In addition there is an excellent pub renowned for its culinary delights and good ale.

The Roof Top Carvery and Coffee Room on the first floor of the Cross Keys has a superb view of the adjacent Minster and it is a most pleasant place to dine. The inn and restaurant on the ground floor are open for lunch and dinner seven days a week, with a three course set lunch on offer from Monday to Friday. The set price menus are changed monthly and the landlord is willing to supply details by post. Starters from the à la carte menu could be puff pastry casket filled with venison in a game sauce, chef's home-made soup, pasta shells served with fresh tomato and a herb and cream sauce or savoury cheese peach, a peach filled with cheese and herb pâté topped with a brandy and mustard crust and grilled. Main courses might be roast loin of pork on a cushion of bramleys, fresh grilled salmon with lobster butter or spring chicken marinated in fresh limes and tarragon. For vegetarians bored with lasagne and cutlets, there are exciting new dishes such as cashew paella, young vegetables in puff pastry with Stilton sauce, and lentil croquettes. There is a selection of sweets from the trolley, all served with fresh cream.

This is a freehouse with a host of traditional hand-pulled real ales – Theakston, Bateman, John Smith's and Ruddles, as well as draught Guinness and cider, two lagers, Foster's and Kronenbourg, and a wide selection of wines. There is a no-smoking area. The Cross Keys is open from 10.30 am to 3 pm and 6 pm to 11 pm. Coffee is served from 10.30 am and food from 12 noon. It is often wise to book in advance for meals. Dogs are not allowed, owing to hygiene regulations.

Telephone: 01427 788314.

How to get there: From Scampton crossroads on the A15, Ermine Street, take the A1500, a long, straight Roman road, as far as Sturton by Stow village and then turn north onto the B1241 for just over a mile. Stow Minster and the Cross Keys are on the left in the village centre.

Parking: There is some parking space in front of the main entrance to the inn, near to the road, with additional parking behind the Cross Keys, at the side of the small lane leading to the Minster. The landlord is quite happy for you to park there while you are doing the walk but requests that you leave a note to that effect.

Length of the walk: 2¹/₂ miles. OS map: Landranger 121 Lincoln and surrounding area (inn GR 883820).

This pleasant stroll takes you over level ground on gentle paths, mostly well-defined, alongside hedges or field headlands. There is a number of stiles en route but all are in good condition. At various stages during the walk attractive views of the ancient church of Stow, said to have been built in AD 678, may be seen and further away the line of the escarpment edge known locally as the Cliff.

The Walk
From the car park at the rear of the Cross Keys walk straight forward, away from the Minster, to cross the lane and take the

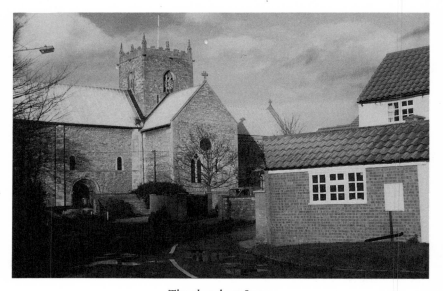

The church at Stow.

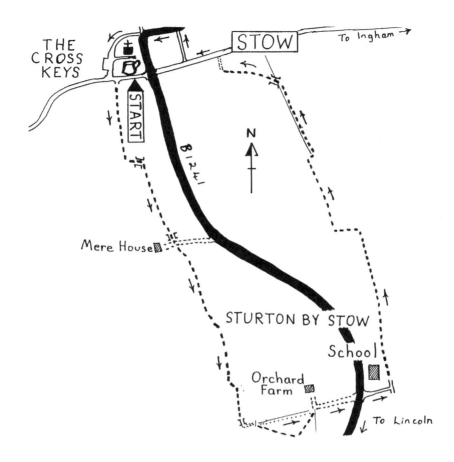

signposted footpath, with the playing field on your immediate left. Follow the dyke round on your left until you reach the wooden footbridge and then continue straight forward towards a dyke and a drive. Turn left for about 25 yards to the footbridge. Cross the drive and climb the stile to head for a double stile in the right-hand corner of the field, with the hedge on your right.

Go through an old iron handgate and continue forward, with the hedge still on the right, to another stile and a waymark by a redundant wooden pylon. Walk diagonally left for 50 yards to the double stile in the fence on your left and then go across the ridge and furrow field. Walk down the field edge, with the hedge on your right, to yet another double stile and a stout footbridge.

Turn left to a metal field gate (waymark) and then walk diagonally right across the field to go through a metal field gate and down the track to the road.

Cross the main road and walk towards the tower of the 1878 Board School, which has the Girls' Entrance now blocked up. Turn left here on a signposted footpath and go over the stile at the side of the metal fieldgate, with the beautifully kept school and playing fields on your immediate left. Follow the field headland round to the left and at the end of the hedge cross over the short distance to the hedge on your right and then walk straight forward, with this hedge now on your left. Both Lincoln Cathedral and Stow Minster are in view here and the line of the Cliff.

Turn left over the footbridge and stile to the bridge and then walk through the young plantation, with a wooden fence on your left. On reaching the lane turn left into the village and turn right down School Lane. At the end of this lane turn left along the grass verge to cross the main road near the bend. Walk straight forward, with the church on your left, until you reach your starting point.

13 Nettleham
The White Hart

A white hart was Richard II's heraldic symbol when he began his reign in 1377 and he insisted that all members of his household wore the device. It would therefore have been a sound move for innkeepers to demonstrate their allegiance by displaying such a highly distinctive visual signal.

Nettleham is an ancient place. There is evidence of occupation by the ancient Britons and in Saxon times the manor belonged to Queen Editha, the wife of Edward the Confessor. Later, it appeared in the Domesday Book as the property of William the Conqueror, who gave its church to an abbey in Normandy. During Roman times two important roads were either side of Nettleham, Ermine Street on its way up to a Humber crossing, and the great Foss Way between Exeter and Saltfleetby on the Lincolnshire coast. Directly opposite the White Hart grassy mounds mark the site of the manor of the bishops of Lincoln who lived here early in the 12th century. A display board indicates the main details of historical interest regarding this site. Today

Nettleham is an attractive and expanding dormitory village not far from the city.

Originally, the White Hart was built as a court house and the former cells are in use today as the beer cellar. Carefully restored and reopened after being totally gutted in a fire, it now has a double lounge with a dining section and, in season, a cheerful open fire at each end. There is a bar parlour with a pool table, juke box and dartboard, plus the Beckside Room in an outbuilding, which is a restaurant capable of seating up to 40 diners. There are tables outside on a small patio area, a separate room where children are welcome and a pleasant south-facing verandah. The beck flows just behind the patio. Dogs are permitted but they must be kept on leads.

This is one of Lincolnshire's own Bateman's houses and serves Dark Mild, XB and Triple XB beers. It also has Tennent's Extra, Marston's Pedigree Bitter and Bass on tap. Scrumpy Jack cider and Murphy's are available, as well as chilled French and German wine. There is a printed menu and an extensive additional range of food is shown on a blackboard. Examples are chicken breast with an apricot and brandy sauce, grilled halibut filled with asparagus, and plaice with a white wine sauce and grapes – and there is always a number of rather splendid desserts. Vegetarian dishes such as tagliatelle niçoise are also served. Meals are available each day from 12 noon to 2.30 pm and from 7 pm to 10 pm. The pub itself is open from 11.30 am (12 noon on Sunday) to 3 pm and from 7 pm to 11 pm.

Telephone: 01522 751976.

How to get there: From the A46 Market Rasen road out of Lincoln turn right 1 mile after the Lincoln bypass roundabout. Nettleham can also be reached by turning off the A158 Lincoln to Horncastle road 2½ miles south-east of the Langworth railway crossing. The White Hart is in the High Street, not far from the church.

Parking: There is parking at the White Hart but it is limited and therefore it is probably better to leave your car at the side of the village green behind the church.

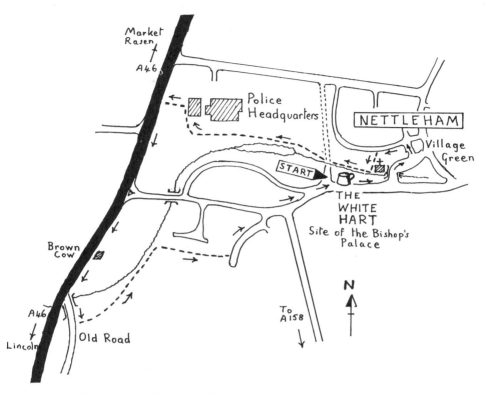

Length of the walk: 2½ miles. OS map: Landranger 121 Lincoln and surrounding area (inn GR 006753).

This is a pleasant, easy walk through a picturesque village and much of the route is on good paths along different stretches of Nettleham Beck, with a ford, a lake and a variety of water birds to be seen. The village green with its attractive sign and a churchyard with an interesting memorial to a murdered postboy, Thomas Gardiner, are visited on the way.

The Walk

From the White Hart cross the road and read the display board information about the site of the Bishop's Palace. Recross to the White Hart side of the High Street and turn right round the bend towards the church, with the beck on your left. On reaching the footbridge after 150 yards turn left into All Saints' churchyard and then to the right back to the road, with the church still on your left. You will find the sad memorial to the young postman to the left of the entrance driveway.

Turn left along Church Street and follow the road round to the green with its splendid village sign. Turn left at the Plough and left again after 150 yards, down All Saints Lane. Turn left at the first turn on the left opposite Linelands, with some bungalows on your right, to follow the curving path round to the right and then go left on the tarmac track back to the side of the beck. Turn right along Beckside, with the beck now on your immediate left, and continue until you reach the ford and Watermill House.

Turn right at the ford for 120 yards until you reach a kissing-gate on your left, which you go through. Please note the warning notice about dogs and do keep to the clear public path through the police grounds. Proceed through the trees to the lake, where seats are provided so that you may sit and admire and try to identify the considerable duck population. Continue along the path to the next kissing-gate and then turn right along the field edge, then left up to the signpost and stile by the main road.

Turn left along to the Washdyke Lane junction and continue straight forward past the Brown Cow on the good tarmac track below the road. Keep on this path past Rose Cottage down to the old road that is now a cul-de-sac. Cross the beck with a deep, tributary, dyke on your left and, at the end of the wooden railings, turn left off the old road onto a signposted public footpath. Follow the clear route diagonally left, at first along the edge of the tributary stream and then alongside the beck itself. On reaching the signpost in the attractive housing estate turn left down Cherry Tree Lane and then left again to Washdyke Lane once more. Turn right down this lane, round the bend and back to the White Hart.

14 Tetford
The White Hart

Another White Hart! The White Hart at Tetford is a gem, too. There is something very special about old hostelries that have welcomed locals and travellers alike throughout the centuries. The inn is said to date from the early 16th century although parts may be older. Almost 200 years later the Tetford Club met here, a social and discussion group that enrolled members of all the neighbouring gentry and many others residing in different parts of the county. Dr Johnson said 'A tavern chair is the throne of human felicity' when he visited in 1764. The old settle in the bar may even have been where Dr Johnson sat. Alfred, Lord Tennyson, from nearby Somersby, was a club member and frequent visitor. His well-known line 'I come from haunts of coot and tern' is said to refer to the infant river Lymn flowing through the village, met at the old water mill during the walk.

Tetford is a figure-of-eight village lying under the wooded uplands of the Wolds and below the Bluestone Heath Road, an ancient saltway following the ridge from the coast – probably the most beautiful road in the county. In the vicinity are extensive encampments supposed to have been constructed during the fighting when the Britons overcame the Saxons, led by Horsa, who were devastating this part of the country. There has been a church here for 900 years although the present building of soft greensand stone dates from the 14th century. There are several interesting memorials, of which the most conspicuous is to Captain Edward Dymoke, who died in 1739. The Dymokes have held the curious hereditary office of the Champion of the King since the time of Richard II. It was the duty of the Champion to ride into Westminster Hall at the coronation feast and, throwing down a gauntlet, to challenge anyone to dispute the king's right to reign. This ceremony has been dispensed with but the Champion now carries the Standard of England at coronations. The Dymokes' Mansion House can be seen during the walk.

The inn is a freehouse serving Mansfield Bitter, Riding Traditional Bitter and a guest beer, changed at irregular intervals. There are two lagers, Red Stripe Strong lager and Carlsberg plus draught Guinness and Scrumpy Jack cider. The bar parlour, with its large oak settle and fireplace, is cosy and full of character, and the refurbished lounge at the front of the house, with fitted banquettes around the bay window, is a delightful, gracious room with an adjoining tiny snug for private conversation. A separate dining room caters for up to 32 diners. There is also a large games/children's room containing a pool table, a piano and satellite television, and fruit drinks are available here from a small bar. The enclosed garden area has a couple of swings and a number of picnic tables. There are five letting rooms for overnight accommodation. No dogs are allowed in the public rooms.

Bar meals range from sandwiches freshly made to order, jacket potatoes with various fillings, ploughman's and burgers to giant Yorkshire puddings, beef or chicken curry, chilli con carne and vegetable or beef lasagne. A selection of lunchtime meals by the French chef is taken from the more extensive evening menu and could include gammon steak, salmon and broccoli mornay, breaded whole scampi tails, home-made steak and kidney or chicken and mushroom pie, lambs' liver and bacon, beef carbonnade cooked in stout, Mediterranean food, which has its own section, or, for vegetarians, bulgar wheat and walnut casserole. There is a special Sunday lunchtime menu, also with a vegetarian dish, and one of the sweets on offer is 'Martin's

The Mansion House at Tetford.

Mum's Home-made Apple Pie'. Children's meals are available or, alternatively, youngsters might like to have an empty plate so that they may share their parents' meal. The pub is open from 12 noon to 3 pm every day except Monday and from 7 pm to 11 pm (10.30 pm on Sunday) each evening with food available throughout these times. This is a popular place and it would always be wise to book in advance for meals at weekends.

Telephone: 01507 533255.

How to get there: Turn off the A153 Horncastle to Louth road at the crossroads by the Wolds Hunt Stables, towards Belchford. Drive up the steep Belchford Hill and turn right along the lovely Bluestone Heath Road for 1½ miles before turning right downhill into Tetford village. Alternatively, turn off the A16(T) Louth to Skegness road to South Ormsby and at the crossroads in that village take the Bluestone Heath Road for almost 3 miles and turn left downhill into Tetford. The White Hart is near the church.

Parking: Some space is available at the White Hart although it is limited and in fairness to the landlord if you intend leaving the

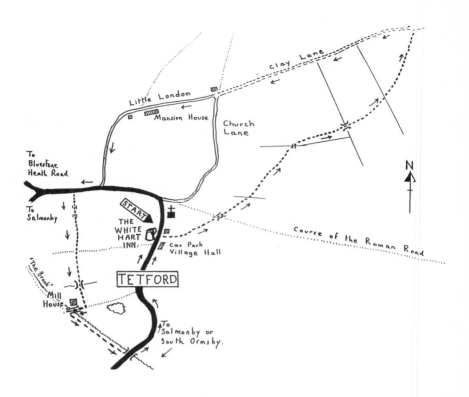

car during your walk it is probably better to park elsewhere. This isn't a problem, for only a few yards away there is the village hall. A member of the village hall committee when asked about the possibility of parking behind it readily agreed and suggested that it would help them to keep the weeds down!

Length of the walk: 2 miles or 3½ miles. OS map: 122 Skegness area (inn GR 332746).

This part of Lincolnshire is a designated Area of Outstanding Natural Beauty (AONB). From the viewpoint on the ancient Bluestone Heath Road, Lincoln Cathedral may be seen some 25 miles away and, looking eastwards, the Lincolnshire coast beloved by Tennyson. He was born in 1809 at Somersby, only a couple of miles from Tetford, and his poems, like Lincolnshire, are full of sky, immense distances and details of nature acutely observed. In the poem 'In Memoriam' he wrote 'Calm and deep peace on this high wold'. An easy walk through quiet countryside with many literary and historical associations – and a superb inn.

The Walk

From the village hall car park turn right to walk the few yards back to the White Hart. From the inn car park cross the road to take the signposted footpath and stile almost directly opposite the front door.

Turn diagonally left at the end of the garden on your left (the footpath originally went straight over this building plot), across the hollow, through the remnant hedge to the stile and footbridge on your left. At the next stile follow the hedge/fence along on the right. There are often English longhorn sheep – a rare breed – in this field. Cross the stile and ditch to turn diagonally left and walk over two fields to a metal field gate and signpost almost in the left-hand corner of the field, by Clay Lane.

Turn left down this green lane, back towards the village. At the road junction, the attractive narrow lane on the left leads you back to the church and the inn for the shorter walk. Otherwise walk straight forward along the lane to Little London, with the Mansion House and the Garth on your left. At the T-junction in the village turn right for 150 yards and then left off the lane on a signposted footpath.

Cross two stiles and then go straight across the arable field on a defined path leading to a concrete footbridge and yet another stile, with the white painted Mill House on your right. On reaching the fence, instead of turning left on a clear path, turn right towards the Mill House and a narrow concrete bridge. Cross the brook and then turn left, with the stream on your immediate left, until you reach the lane. Turn left on the lane, go over the road bridge and round the bends in the road, back to your starting point.

Places of interest nearby

Some 5 miles from Tetford, *Stockwith Mill*, between Bag Enderby and Hagworthingham is worth a visit. It is mentioned by Tennyson in his poem *The Brook*. The buildings, which are 18th century, are now used as a restaurant and craft shop and there are three waymarked short walks nearby. Open from 10.30 am to 6 pm on Tuesday to Sunday from Easter to October. Telephone: 01507 588221.

15 Tetney Lock
The Crown and Anchor

The Crown and Anchor is the badge of the Lord High Admiral and also the arm badge of petty officers in the Royal Navy. It symbolises the fidelity of sailors to the monarchy. Retired seamen who became licensees were often fond of the name for their hostelries.

In 1704 an enterprising Dutchman, the captain of a sloop, bought an acre of land alongside the river Lud and built on it a warehouse and an inn, now the Crown and Anchor. Smuggling was rife in the area at the time, both outward and inward, when soaring customs duties on tea, spirits, tobacco and silk turned 'freetrading' into a large and lucrative industry. Few ships sailed from Tetney Haven, Saltfleet or Grainthorpe without a bale or two of wool in the hold. The Humber entrance has vast, open, sandy beaches where, in good weather, boats could run up out of the water or, alternatively, casks or barrels could be thrown overboard to float gently ashore on the rising tide. Smuggling required the co-operation of many local people for storage, transport and distribution, and a secret staircase was discovered in the Crown and Anchor during renovation work in the 1960s. The coastguard cottages at Tetney were built in 1842 and a full patrol was carried out every night of the year, except for the first five nights of the full moon when half the detachment was allowed to rest. In 1767 Louth was linked to the North Sea by straightening the river Lud and creating an 11¾ mile canal but its chief drawback was its difficult entrance from the sea at Tetney Haven. However, it was successful in the early years, importing coal and timber and exporting corn and wool, until it was bought by the East Lincolnshire Railway Co, in 1847. The pub did well catering for the Irish navvies who built the canal and later for customers from the barges.

Today the Crown and Anchor is a trim, white-painted, canalside freehouse. There isn't a village and nowadays the canal traffic has disappeared, but it offers hospitality to a diverse clientele consisting of farmers, fishermen, walkers, wildfowlers, bird watchers and caravanners. The low-beamed bar parlour has a pool table and a dartboard, an assortment of stuffed animals and birds, and guns and a rod in the Wildfowlers' Corner. At the side of the pub there is a pleasant, light and airy lounge bar with comfortable bench seating and, outside, you will find picnic tables at the front of the pub and at the rear. Regular musical entertainment is a feature. There is a caravan park for four caravans with shower block and toilet, a beer garden and a play area for children, who are allowed in the pub until 8 pm. Dogs are not permitted in the lounge bar, where food is served. During the winter months splendid home-made soup is dished up to combat the chill of the east winds off the sea. Good value, simple bar food is available almost whenever the pub is open – ham and chips, ploughman's, salads, baps with various fillings and hot dishes such as chicken, fish, scampi or pies. There is a traditional roast lunch on a Sunday, for which it might be advisable to book in advance. As for drinks, well-kept Stone's Bitter on handpump and Bass Draught and Mild, Carling Black Label and draught Guinness are on offer. The opening times are 12 noon to 3 pm every lunchtime and 6 pm to 11 pm in the evening (7 pm to 10.30 pm on Sunday).
Telephone: 01472 388291.

How to get there: Tetney Lock is a hamlet at the end of the road with only the marsh beyond, except for a little lane leading to North Cotes. Southbound, turn off the A1031 Cleethorpes to Mablethorpe road in Tetney and continue for 2 miles to Tetney Lock. Northbound, turn off the A1031 Mablethorpe to Cleethorpes road just beyond Marshchapel, going through North Cotes to Tetney Lock. From the A16(T) Grimsby to Louth road, turn onto the B1201 at North Thoresby and then proceed either via Tetney or North Cotes.

Parking: The pub has a large car park for up to 60 cars and the landlord is quite willing for walkers to leave their cars there during the walk. Alternative parking for individual cars may be found on the roadside across the canal, either by the pumping station or by the old chapel.

Length of the walk: 2½ miles. OS map: Landranger 113 Grimsby and surrounding area (inn GR 344021).

Here is a smugglers' coast, a wide marsh that is an important nature reserve. In contrast, there is a view of two World War I forts built to protect the Humber mouth from enemy attack and a high-tech oil terminal capable of pumping millions of gallons of crude to Tetney Tank Farm. In winter strong winds off the sea can be bitter but most exhilarating, for this is one of our county's too few wild places – unknown to many who have lived in Lincolnshire all their days.

The Walk

Turn right out of the pub car park, with the Louth Canal on your immediate left, to proceed along the signposted public footpath. At the field gate climb the rather awkward sloping stile and then follow the wide track along the top of the embankment or, if you want to shelter from the wind, walk below the embankment by the waterside.

At the next stile continue forward until you reach the World War II concrete machine gun post and then turn left to the field gate and stile to cross the concrete lock gates and bridge at the canal entrance.

Tetney Haven Bird Reserve, stretching ahead, forms an

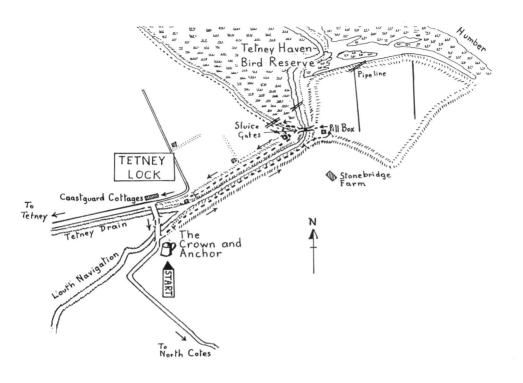

important feeding area in the mouth of the estuary and a large number and variety of wildfowl and waders can be seen here on migration and in winter. Gulls roost on the sandbars in immense numbers and skuas are frequent in autumn. The large breeding colony of the scarce little tern is of special interest, and there are also significant breeding populations of shelduck, oystercatchers, ringed plovers and redshanks.

The Tetney monobuoy lies about 3 miles offshore, the first to be installed in British waters. It is held in position by eight anchors and tankers are moored to it, connected with floating hoses. Oil is pumped along the 36 inch pipeline to your right, to the eight storage tanks at Tetney, which have a capacity of 2 million barrels. The two forts in the distance, Haile Sand Fort and the larger Bull Fort, had an anti-submarine steel mesh net stretched between them. The first British Army casualties

Tetney Lock.

of World War II occurred here when a German mine-laying aeroplane machine-gunned the forts, which held garrisons of up to 200 men.

At the National Rivers Authority outfall notice leave this good track and walk straight forward for about 80 yards to then turn left along the clear public right of way, with a deep drain on your immediate right.

At the concrete machine gun post turn right on the track again (the track is private only for the first 150 yards) and walk down the canalside, ignoring the track where it turns to the right. Climb the stile and remain on the canal bank almost until you reach the road bridge past the old chapel. At the road turn left over the bridge, back to your starting place.

16 Redbourne
The Red Lion

About a mile after turning off the Roman Ermine Street, these days the A15(T), one comes to Redbourne village, quieter now that the trunk road has been connected to the M180 Scunthorpe roundabout. The village has charm, with ducks swimming on the wayside stream and often invading the car park, a fine stone gateway at the entrance to Redbourne Park and a wide village green on the bend in the road, with the Red Lion nestling neatly behind, a little way from the through highway.

This is an old-fashioned, half-timbered coaching inn with unspecified Nell Gwynne connections. An attractive side garden offers outside seating throughout the summer and there are additional tables at the front, overlooking the tree-clad green. An interesting old fire station adjoins the inn by the courtyard entrance. There is a long front bar with tapestry bench seating, some fascinating little alcoves and a small bay-windowed room adjoining. The pool room has a juke box, darts and television. There are also twelve bedrooms and a large restaurant.

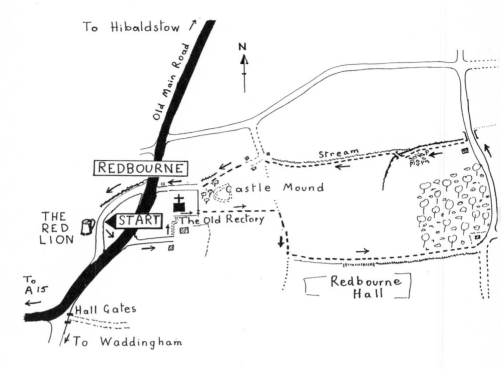

A freehouse, the inn serves Stones Bitter, Bass Mild and Special Bitter, Worthington Best Bitter and Tennent's Extra, as well as Carling Black Label and Tennent's Pilsner lager, draught Guinness and Dry Blackthorn cider. It is open for drinks all day from 11 am to 11 pm on Monday to Saturday, and on Sunday from 12 noon to 3 pm and 7 pm to 10.30 pm. The Red Lion bar food includes soup, sandwiches, ploughman's and simple but filling hot dishes such as steak and kidney pie, gammon and steaks, scampi and lasagne, and the restaurant provides a more extensive range. On Sunday there is a special three-course lunch as well as the usual bar meals. Food is available each day from 12 noon to 2.15 pm and 7.15 pm to 10 pm. Dogs are permitted only when meals are not being served, because of hygiene regulations.

Telephone: 01652 648302.

How to get there: Turn eastwards off the A15(T) Scunthorpe to Lincoln road, 6 miles north of the Caenby Corner roundabout

(5 miles south of the M180 Scunthorpe roundabout). The lane is signposted 'Redbourne'.

Parking: There is concealed additional parking through the entrance into the old courtyard by the fire station but the majority of visitors park on the very adequate car park in front of the inn, overlooking the village green.

Length of the walk: 2 miles. OS map: Landranger 112 Scunthorpe and surrounding area (inn GR 972999).

This circuit from the peaceful village of Redbourne takes you over pleasant field paths and an empty lane and returns you alongside a little stream, with the former blacksmith's forge and stocks for wrongdoers by the roadside. Nothing remains today of Redbourne Castle except some grassy mounds and a dry moat, seen en route. The Dukes of St Albans once lived at Redbourne Park with its fine stone gateway and lion crest. There are still many fine trees in and around the park, whose wall you follow on this gentle, level walk.

The Walk

Cross the main road to follow the signposted footpath on the right pointing along Church Lane. At the end of the lane turn left to follow the waymark round the edge of the recreation area and then the graveyard to a newly constructed kissing-gate in the churchyard wall.

Walk straight across the arable field to turn right on meeting another footpath, along the field edge, keeping the dyke on your immediate left. At the end of the field by the hall grounds turn left on good track, with the grounds and wall on your right, and continue forward until you arrive at Gingerbread Cottage on the left.

Turn left here and left again within a few yards on reaching the lane, with some lovely mature trees on both sides. By the house on the left immediately before the road bridge turn left off the road on a signposted path, with the stream on your right. Continue forward through the small thicket until you meet the wooden footbridge with a handrail. Cross the bridge and turn left along the field edge, with another stream on your right. At the footpath

Old smithy and stocks, Redbourne.

signpost and bridge turn right for a few yards to the lane, with the Anglian Water Pumping Station on your right.

Turn left down the lane, with Hawkstone House on the left, and follow the attractive path straight forward, with a tall hedge on your left, into School Lane, with Brook Cottage on the right. The school has gone now and the building has been converted into a house. Cross the main road and turn left, with the stream now on your right and the picnic tables on the village green over on the left, back to your starting place.

17 Laceby
The Waterloo/The Nag's Head

A most unusual two-pub pub. They are in the Guinness Book of Records as the two closest-built pubs, separate outside and as one inside. They were combined a few years ago when one became vacant. Customers must use separate doors to enter either pub but the bar is the connecting link serving both pubs.

Ley lines are supposed to join settlements or important points of long ago on lines of magnetic bearings. There are two possible ley lines crossing at Laceby so perhaps giving the village its name 'settlement at a boundary or crossing point'. The old route from Grimsby to Caistor passed through the Square where the annual Statute fair used to be held up until World War I. The most famous rector of the late Norman church of St Margaret's in Laceby was John Whitgift, who became Archbishop of Canterbury in 1583 during the reign of Elizabeth I and lived to place the crown on the head of James I. The church register tells of the execution of a witch in 1546 who was 'devoured' by fire.

The Waterloo with its elegant lounge and family room has

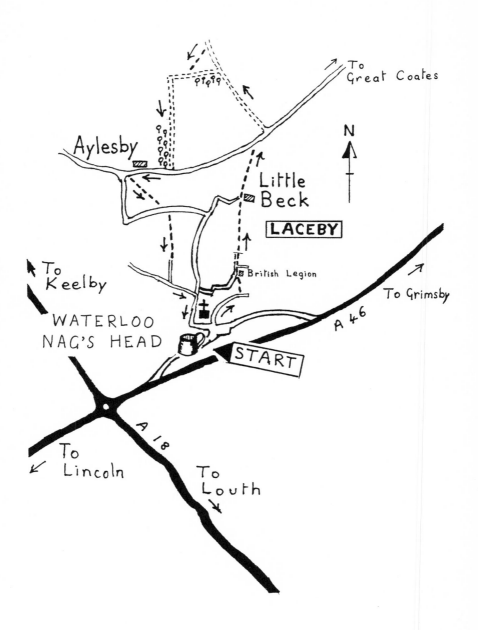

To Great Coates

Aylesby

N

Little Beck

LACEBY

To Keelby

British Legion

To Grimsby

WATERLOO
NAG'S HEAD

A 46

START

A 18

To Lincoln

To Louth

a most attractive decor – brass footrails, comfortable leather banquettes, a carpeted restaurant and a prevailing brown that is altogether pleasing. The Nag's Head is very much more basic, offering friendly service in a pleasant bar-parlour atmosphere. There is a family room, a no-smoking section and well-behaved dogs are permitted. There is a constantly changing, very extensive blackboard menu and an incredibly good-value three-course meal consisting of, for example, a starter course of soup or egg mayonnaise, 6 oz gammon, chips and peas or chicken pie, chips and a vegetable, and apple pie and custard. A wide variety of sandwiches can be made to order and there are basket meals, jacket potatoes with various fillings, steak and kidney pie and home-made lasagne. The pubs serve Bass Mild, Bass, Worthington Best Bitter, Thomas Caffrey's Irish Ale and Stones Best Bitter (keg), plus quite a range of wine. The opening times on Monday to Saturday are from 11 am to 11 pm, and on Sunday from 12 noon to 3 pm and 7 pm to 10.30 pm.
Telephone: 01472 874961.

How to get there: Turn off the A46 Lincoln to Grimsby road into the village 500 yards on the Grimsby side of the Laceby roundabout. The Waterloo/Nag's Head is/are on the left of the village square.

Parking: There is free parking on the village square directly in front of the pubs or in their own car park to the rear.

Length of the walk: 3 miles. OS map: Landranger 113 Grimsby and surrounding area (inn GR 213065).

This leisurely walk takes you through the village for a short distance and then across farmland on good public footpaths and tracks, over level ground, passing en route a fine, gabled block of dwellings with dormer windows looking out over beautiful gardens, the almshouses at Aylesby.

The Walk
From Laceby village square turn left along Church Lane and left again at Stockwell end to go through the small green with a wooden fence on the left and a chapel across the road at the

The church at Laceby.

end of Waterloo Terrace.

Turn right past the British Legion and where the road turns right continue straight forward on a good track to the stile and fingerpost, then past the small bend to the left and on to the lane, with a hedge now on your right.

At the lane turn right for a few yards and then left up a good, signposted track after crossing the dyke. There is a storebuilding on the right and you continue forward along the track, with the hedge on your immediate left. After about 500 yards, at the end of the small wood on the left, turn left on a good track. After some 350 yards turn left, again on a good track, back towards the lane.

Upon reaching the lane turn right towards Aylesby village, past the splendid almshouse on your right. This was erected in memory of a 25 year old Royal Field Artillery Captain, Francis McAuley, who fell in action in France, in 1916. At the T-junction turn diagonally left across the field to the lane and, almost opposite, follow the clear, signposted footpath leading eventually into a little lane, where you turn left and then right towards the church and your starting place.

18 Bottesford
The Beckwood

The Beckwood is quite different from all the other hostelries in the book in that it is a comparatively recently built housing estate pub, but it is certainly no less welcoming to walkers. Although Bottesford has gradually grown into a suburb of Scunthorpe, its old centre retains its village character and even today the church still looks out on open country.

The inn has an attractive, airy lounge bar with large windows, comfortable banquette seating and interesting local pictures on the walls. The bar parlour has a pool table, dartboard and television. In front of the pub there is a grass area on a mound with a couple of picnic tables. A Whitbread tenancy, it serves a range of real ales, including Whitbread Best Bitter, Trophy Bitter, Castle Eden Ale and Abbot Ale. There are two lagers, Stella Artois and Heineken, and two ciders, Woodpecker and Addlestone's Cask Conditioned. Draught Guinness is also on offer. The opening times are from 12 noon to 11 pm on Friday and Saturday, 12 noon to 3 pm and 5.30 pm to 11 pm on Monday to Thursday, and from 12 noon to

3 pm and 7 pm to 10.30 pm on Sunday.

The comprehensive menu includes 'Breakfast Anytime', burgers, filled jacket potatoes, Holme Hall ploughman's and omelettes. Appetisers include country soup, prawn cocktail, hot mushrooms and fruit cup. From the garden there is vegetable lasagne, vegetarian mixed grill and broccoli and cheese bake. Specialities include steak and ale pie, home-made lasagne and 'The Great British Tradition' – Grimsby haddock, chips, peas and salad garnish. Food is served every day from 12 noon to 2 pm and there is a special Sunday lunch menu. Evening meals are available on Thursday, Friday and Saturday, from 6 pm to 8 pm.

Telephone: 01724 856342.

How to get there: Turn off the A159 Scunthorpe to Gainsborough road at the crossroads $1/2$ mile north of the bridge over the Bottesford Beck and then go right at the crossroads in the 'village'. After another $1/2$ mile the Beckwood is round the bend on the left. Alternatively, Bottesford can be reached from the B1398, which runs south from the A18, not far from junction 4 on the M180. In which case, the Beckwood will be found at the foot of the hill on the right as you enter the suburbs.

Parking: There is ample parking at the Beckwood and the landlord is quite agreeable for walkers' cars to be left there. Alternative roadside parking is available, with care, off the main road.

Length of the walk: $1^3/4$ miles. OS map: Landranger 112 Scunthorpe and surrounding area (inn GR 903073).

This pleasant stroll is an interesting exploration of a village that has grown and includes a glimpse of a fascinating old well. Bottesford Beck has been made into a linear country park and the walk follows some of this waterside route. Holme Lane has some attractive houses and gardens and the development of the new housing includes designed walkways that demonstrate what can be done with imagination and forethought.

The Walk

Walk down the steps leading from the front of the pub to the road and turn left downhill. Cross the road to turn right up

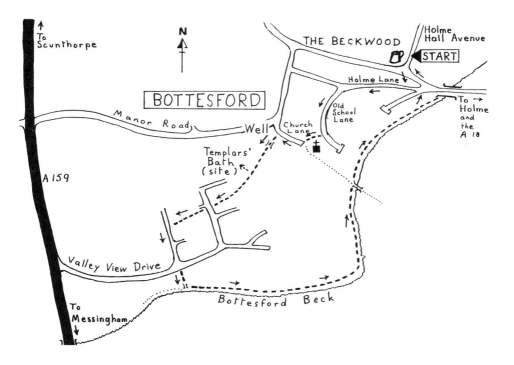

Holme Lane. Turn left up Old School Lane to St Peter's church, around 800 years old. Its full title is a most unusual dedication to St Peter ad Vincula (St Peter in Chains) – another church in England with this name may be found in the Tower of London. Go through the metal entrance gates and walk up the church path to the other entry on Church Lane, where there is a handgate and a footpath signpost.

In Church Lane there is a hut-like structure in the stone wall of the first house at the top of the lane. It has wrought iron gates and if you peep through them you will see that the structure is full of water and that it is what the locals called St John's Well. Legend has it that the Knights Templar used the water for washing before undertaking a vigil in the church before going off to the Crusades in the Holy Land. The actual well is situated in the front garden of the house, which is named after the well and the level of the water is said never to change even in very dry periods. The outside 'hut' on the road is the overflow from the well. The people of

Bottesford Beck.

Bottesford were entitled to use water in the case of drought for the sum of one penny per bucket. The Templars' Bath close by the well filled up with mud 100 years ago.

By Hardwick Villa, on the left of Church Lane, take the signposted path and in a few yards cross the narrow footbridge with a handrail. Continue forward on a clear path and on reaching an estate road go straight across to turn left downhill on Worcester Close, the next road along.

Cross Valley View Road and go through the kissing-gate on the signposted path leading down to the beck. Turn left at the wooden footbridge, with the beck on your immediate right. Continue along the side of the beck until you come almost to Holme Lane and then turn diagonally left across the grass to walk uphill, back to your starting place.

19 Stallingborough
The Green Man

The Green Man sign is associated with Robin Hood and his men, who were reputed to be dressed in Lincoln Green cloth. This was a light green material made in Lincoln and it was used for the clothing of foresters, woodmen and the like from the 16th century onwards. The Green Man was also associated with the pagan May Day celebrations at the beginning of spring.

The Green Man belies its roadside appearance. Extensions have been well done and they have created a most pleasant venue. The grounds at the rear are quite extensive and children may play in view and with safety for there is better than average play equipment with protective surfaces. A patio with picnic tables is situated on the edge of this pleasant, grassy area and glass doors from the lounge bar overlook it. The lounge is a most attractive room, well carpeted and with comfortable banquette seating around the walls and internal divisions of the large area to promote private grouping. It has big windows, framed pictures and there are brick supporting pillars and some unusual carvings.

The bar parlour provides a contrast and has a pool table, darts and television. On the wall there is an unusual and interesting display of different calibre bullets, from Colts to Mausers.

From Monday to Saturday the Green Man is open all day from 11.30 am to 11 pm. On Sunday it is open from 12 noon to 3 pm and from 7 pm to 10.30 pm.

There are four cask ales on handpump, Worthington Best Bitter, Stones Bitter, Bass and Thomas Caffrey's Irish Ale. The two lagers on offer are Carling Black Label and Tennent's Pilsner. There is also draught Guinness, Blackthorn cider and a range of wines by the glass or the bottle. The bar food includes baked potatoes with a choice of five tasty fillings, burgers, battered chicken steak, a choice of six salad platters and, for vegetarians, meat-free lasagne, mushroom stroganoff, harvester's pie, tomato and vegetable tagliatelle or cheese and broccoli quiche. A blackboard menu offers a daily choice of freshly cooked seasonal dishes. Starters might be crispy vegetable platter, breaded mushrooms or deep fried prawns. Main course dishes range from mixed grill, chicken, gammon and mushroom pie and grilled pork chop to fillet of haddock or Scottish salmon fillet. Chocolate fudge cake or passion cake could be among the delicious sounding desserts. There is a special three-course Sunday lunch but the bar menu remains available. Food is served at lunchtime every day from 12 noon to 2 pm. Evening meals are from 7 pm to 9.30 pm on Tuesday to Thursday (no food on Friday evening), to 10 pm on Saturday and to 9 pm on Sunday and Monday.

Telephone: 01472 883464.

How to get there: From the A1173 Caistor to Immingham road turn off at Stallingborough roundabout, 2½ miles north of the Riby crossroads. The Green Man is 400 yards north of the railway crossing gates.

Parking: Ample parking is available at the Green Man and the landlord is quite willing for walkers to leave their cars providing they patronise the pub. There is very little alternative parking in the immediate vicinity.

Length of the walk: 2½ miles. OS map: Landranger 113 Grimsby and surrounding area (inn GR 205118).

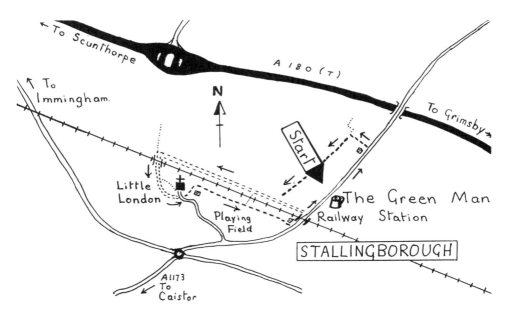

This is an easy walk, partly up the village street but mainly on good field paths to an isolated brick built church, replacing an older one that fell down in the 18th century. There was once a manor and village to the north and west of the church. Little London (lundr) is Old Norse for a sacred grove. Is this where King Offa once held court? Colonel Harrison, a Roundhead officer killed at the Battle of Riby Gap in 1645, lies buried in the churchyard here along with some of his soldiers. The walk takes you alongside a Lincolnshire rarity – a working railway with a station. One section of the walk has an extraordinary number of stiles and footbridges, all in good order.

The Walk
Turn right down Marsh Lane on leaving the Green Man, for about 200 yards. Turn left off the road along the good green, signposted track, with the deep dyke on the left. This is a section of the Nev Cole Way, a long-distance recreational path in memory of a well loved rambler who walked these paths all his days.

A working railway!

Turn left along the field edge, with the stream on your left. Cross the small wooden bridge with a handrail to turn right on the wide track, with the railway on the left. Turn left through both wooden field gates on crossing the railway line and do please remember to close them. Follow the track towards the church and near the entrance cross the stile by the signpost on the left to turn right on the tarmac church path for about 60 yards. Turn right for a few yards and where the track bends to the right continue straight forward, with a high brick wall on the right.

Follow the path over six stiles and footbridge, with a playing field on your right until you reach a kissing-gate on the main road. Turn left up the road, over the railway crossing by the station, past Bluebell Cottage on the right and back to the pub car park.

Places of interest nearby

National Fishing Heritage Centre, Alexandra Dock, Great Grimsby. Telephone: 01472 344867.

20 Bonby
The Haymaker

Bonby is one of a string of spring-line villages on the western edge of the Wolds, overlooking the wide plain down to the Humber. A priory was founded here in the time of King John as a cell of the Carthusian abbey of St Fromard in Normandy. However, parts of the church are even older, with two doorways dating from the Saxon period. One short section of the walk is along a lane now part of a South Humberside Scenic Drive, clinging closely to the cliff edge where it follows the prehistoric ridgeway far older than the parallel Roman road. This ancient route runs all the way down to the Lincoln Gap and then beyond through Lincolnshire into the Cotswolds.

The Haymaker is quite a discovery, although it is an ordinary looking house with a considerable extension at the rear. It used to be called Pandora's Box but, on change of ownership, became the Haymaker, aptly named because of the amount of rural activity in the immediate vicinity. Nestling at the roadside in the main street of Bonby village, this is an unpretentious pub with two simply furnished bars. One of these is a typical bar parlour with pool table, darts and jukebox. The other, the lounge bar, is a light, pleasant room with a small dining area that becomes a restaurant at weekends. This lounge bar offers a welcoming atmosphere in which to enjoy good food – and it really is good. A simple set meal at an extraordinarily reasonable price, perhaps soup or pâté, roast meat and vegetables, and a choice of sweet, is offered on Friday and Saturday evenings, and a four-course lunch on Sunday. Booking is advisable, though, for the number of diners is restricted to 25. The proprietress prepares all the food personally and emphasis is on quality. At other times bar food is on offer but it would still be wise to confirm availability in advance. A chip shop is open in another section of the pub on Wednesday, Thursday and Friday evenings. Outside, there is a patio area with picnic tables and a play area for children. A freehouse, the Haymaker serves three lagers, Heineken, Stella Artois and Carlsberg Export, two ciders, Strongbow and Addlestone's Cask Conditioned on handpump, draught Guinness, Whitbread Trophy Bitter, Eden Bitter plus one guest beer, changing regularly. The pub is closed on Monday and Tuesday, and on the other days the opening times are from 12 noon to 2 pm (4 pm on Saturday) and 7 pm to 11 pm, and on Sunday from 12 noon to 3 pm and 7 pm to 10.30 pm.

Telephone: 01652 618793.

How to get there: Bonby is on the B1204 South Ferriby to Elsham road. It is 3½ miles north of Elsham and 4 miles south of South Ferriby. Elsham is signposted on a minor road from the Barnetby roundabout off the Grimsby to Scunthorpe motorway, the M180.

Parking: There is adequate parking at the Haymaker, otherwise roadside parking, with care, along the village street.

Length of the walk: 2 miles. OS map: Landranger 112 Scunthorpe and surrounding area (inn GR 002153).

This easy walk on quiet lanes and good paths offers fine views over the flatlands known as the Carrs, down to the Humber and the New Ancholme. Surely one of the best sections of the Tourist

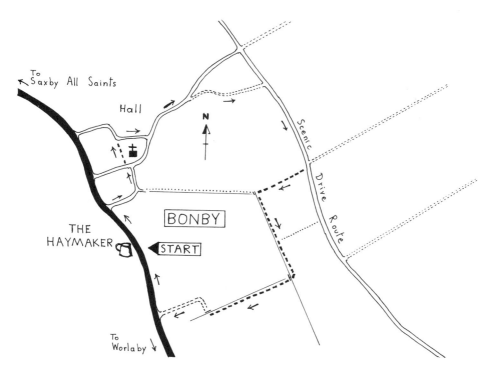

Board's 40-mile scenic drive route must be the ancient, cliff-edge, narrow lane above Bonby. The walk uses this lane for about 350 yards before joining a cross-field path leading downhill into Bonby village. There is one quite steep stretch on the lane above Bonby church.

The Walk

Turn left out of the pub car park along Main Street, with the tiny Methodist chapel on your right. Turn right up Sheepdyke Lane and follow the lane round to St Andrew's church. Have a look under the lychgate canopy, then go through the churchyard, turning left along the tarmac path to Hall Meadow.

Turn right up the road to the T-junction and then left uphill, using the footpath through the trees on the left in order to keep off the steep, narrow road. Where this path ends cross the road to follow the ancient holloway track leading uphill to the escarpment edge lane.

The road to Bonby church.

Turn right along this lane for 350 yards, and directly opposite a track on the left, turn off the lane to the right on a signposted footpath leading downhill across the field for about 200 yards. Upon reaching the hedge turn left, with a hedge on your immediate right, until you meet a stile. Go over the stile and proceed downhill through the attractive little valley, with a hedge still on your right. By the house on the right turn right over the next stile for a few yards and then left down the good track to the road.

Turn right at the road down Main Street, back to the Haymaker, passing Freeman's Lane on your right en route.

Places of interest nearby
Elsham Hall Country and Wildlife Park, to the south, has a falconry centre, a craft and garden centre, lakeside gardens, an adventure playground, an animal farm, a pets' corner and a restaurant and tearooms. Telephone: 01652 688698.